Contents

Contributors v

1. **Introduction** *Jennifer Harrison and Janet Edwards* 1

2. **Setting the Scene** *Jennifer Harrison* 8

3. **The Health of the Nation: A Strategic Framework** ....
   Gillian Morgan 23

4. **The Process and Practice of Health Education** 39
   Counselling Skills in the Classroom *Sylvia McNamara* 39
   Active Learning Strategies *Neil Kitson* 47
   The Role of Recording Achievement *David Tomley* 52

5. **Health Education and the Cross-Curricular Themes** 56
   Economic and Industrial Understanding *Alan Sutton* 56
   Careers Education and Guidance *Graham Robb* 60
   Citizenship Education *Ken Fogelman* 65
   Environmental Education *Steve Goodall* 70

6. **Health Education and Other Subjects in the Curriculum** 74
   Mathematics *Rose Griffiths* 74
   Science *Jennifer Harrison* 79
   English *Ros McCulloch* 84
   History *David Kerr* 88
   Geography *Patrick Bailey* 92
   Design and Technology *Tina Jarvis* 96
   Modern Languages *Wasyl Cajkler* 101
   Art *Martin Wenham* 105
   Physical Education *Angela Wortley* 110
   Music *Linda Hargreaves* 115
   Religious Education *Mark Lofthouse* 120
   Social Sciences and Sociology *Tony Lawson* 125

7. **Equal Opportunities in Health Education** 129
   Special Educational Needs *Sylvia McNamara* 129
   Gender Issues *Mel Vlaeminke* 133

iv

Developing Health Education In and For a Multi-cultural
Society *Pauline Hoyle* 137

8. The Role of the Community in Health Education 142
The Health Professionals *Alison Timmins* 142
The Role of Health Promotion *Marilyn Stephens and
Hugh Graham* 147
Governors and Parents *Ann Holt* 152
The Influence of the Media *Roger Dickinson* 158

Index 162

Developing Health Education in the Curriculum

Edited by
**Jennifer Harrison and
Janet Edwards**

David Fulton Publishers
London

David Fulton Publishers Ltd
2 Barbon Close, London WC1N 3JX

First published in Great Britain by
David Fulton Publishers 1994

Note: The right of Jennifer Harrison and Janet Edwards to be identified as the Editors of this work has been asserted by them in accordance with the Copyright, Designs and Patents Act 1988.

British Library Cataloguing in Publication Data

A catalogue record for this book is available from the British Library

ISBN 1-85346-277-2

Typeset by Textype Typesetters, Cambridge
Printed in Great Britain by BPC Journals, Exeter

Contributors

Bailey, Patrick
Consultant in Education, Trustee of the Geographical Association, University of Leicester

Cajkler, Wasyl
Lecturer, School of Education, University of Leicester

Dickinson, Roger
Lecturer, Centre for Mass Communication Research, University of Leicester

Edwards, Janet
Deputy Director of the Centre for Citizenship Studies in Education, School of Education, University of Leicester

Fogelman, Ken
Professor and Director of the Centre for Citizenship Studies in Education, School of Education, University of Leicester

Goodall, Steve
Headteacher, Old Stratford County Primary School, Milton Keynes

Graham, Hugh
Health Promotion Manager, East Sussex Health Authority

Griffiths, Rose
Lecturer, School of Education, University of Leicester

Hargreaves, Linda
Lecturer, School of Education, University of Leicester

Harrison, Jennifer
Lecturer, School of Education, University of Leicester

Holt, Ann
Director, Christians in Education, 53 Romney Street, London

Hoyle, Pauline
Science Inspector, Islington Education Department, London

Jarvis, Tina
Lecturer, School of Education, University of Leicester

Kerr, David	Lecturer, School of Education, University of Leicester
Kitson, Neil	Lecturer, School of Education, University of Leicester
Lawson, Tony	Lecturer, School of Education, University of Leicester
Lofthouse, Mark	Senior Lecturer, School of Education, University of Leicester
McCulloch, Ros	Lecturer, School of Education, University of Leicester
McNamara, Sylvia	Lecturer, School of Education, University of Leicester
Morgan, Gillian	Director of Public Health, Fosse Health Trust, Leicester
Robb, Graham	Headteacher, Lode Heath School, Solihull
Stephens, Marilyn	Advisory Teacher (Sexual Health), East Sussex Advisory and Inspection Service
Sutton, Alan	Lecturer, School of Education, University of Leicester
Timmins, Alison	Senior Nurse (Research), Fosse Health Trust Headquarters, Leicester
Tomley, David	Senior Lecturer, School of Education, University of Leicester
Vlaeminke, Mel	Lecturer, School of Education, University of Leicester
Wenham, Martin	Lecturer, School of Education, University of Leicester
Wortley, Angela	Director of Physical Education, Lecturer, School of Education, University of Leicester

CHAPTER 1

Introduction

Jennifer Harrison and Janet Edwards

A fundamental statement from the 1988 Education Reform Act, placed a statutory responsibility upon schools to provide a broad and balanced curriculum which 'promotes the spiritual, moral, cultural, mental and physical development of pupils at the school and of society' and prepares pupils 'for the responsibilities, opportunities and experiences of adult life'.

More specific reference to breadth and balance in the curriculum appeared in *Curriculum Guidance 3: The Whole Curriculum* (NCC, 1990), which set the context for developing the school curriculum and explained that the 'basic curriculum' (core and foundation subjects and RE) can form the foundation but will not, on its own, provide the necessary breadth. It should be 'augmented by additional subjects, an accepted range of cross-curricular elements and extra-curricular activities'. In addition there will be 'intangibles which come from the spirit and ethos of each school, its pupils and staff, teaching methods, management of the curriculum and of the school'.

Cross-curricular elements were described as:

- **dimensions** – which give equality of opportunity to all pupils, and take account of diversity of gender, cultural and linguistic background, and special educational needs;

- **skills**
  - communication;
  - numeracy;
  - study;
  - problem solving;
  - personal and social;
  - information technology;

- **themes**
  - economic and industrial understanding;
  - careers education and guidance;
  - health education;
  - education for citizenship;
  - environmental education.

The NCC has published curriculum guidance on each of these five themes, but as Edwards and Fogelman (1993) noted:

> 'Coherence in the curriculum was one of the principles upon which the Education Reform Act was based. However, the way in which the subject and cross-curricular documents emerged from the National Curriculum Council lacked coherence. There is a risk that pupils will see their learning as a series of discrete experiences unless teachers and community partners work together to make sense of the curriculum jig-saw (see, for example, Hargreaves, 1991). There is a real opportunity to use the cross-curricular elements as a constructive way forward towards ensuring entitlement and coherence in the learning experiences of all pupils.'

In Chapter 3 of *Developing Citizenship in the Curriculum* the planning process is addressed and the authors (Harrison and Knights) draw on work with Leicestershire teachers in all phases. Only with considerable effort and skill will coherence for the pupil be achieved. This volume does not repeat this curriculum planning advice but rather invites the reader to consider the series of books as a whole.

We, in working on this book, have been helped in our thinking about development planning by Dy Shepherd, who was a member of a Leicestershire team that produced county guidelines for health education under the title *Working Together for Health – guidelines for a whole school/college approach*. 'The curriculum planning process consists of four main processes:

- an audit (a school/college review, its strengths and areas for development);
- plan construction (priorities for development are selected and then turned into specific targets);
- implementation;
- evaluation.

Successful curriculum development of health education requires that all staff, pupils, parents, and governors share a clear understanding of the primary aims and objectives of health education. Only by health education messages being reinforced by the whole school community will real health progress be assured.'

> 'The National Curriculum Council did not follow the curriculum guidance documents with any INSET advice for whole curriculum planning and we are aware that without such guidance the task is sometimes perceived by schools as almost too difficult to contemplate. The NCC produced in March 1992, three working papers entitled *Setting the scene: commonality in the cross-curricular themes, Overview of the cross-curricular themes* and *Equal opportunities and ERA*' (Edwards and Fogelman, 1993).

Publications addressing the issues of integration and coherence across the whole curriculum are rare, but include INSET packs from Pearson Publishing (Edwards and Pathan, 1993, and, with specific reference to this theme, Harrison, 1993).

'If the cross-curricular elements are to permeate the curriculum an essential pre-requisite seems to us to be that those responsible for the implementation of the core and foundation subjects should consider the relationship between their own subjects and the themes' (Edwards and Fogelman, 1993).

This book aims to facilitate the understanding of health education and its relationship with other curriculum areas. Written as it is by those with special knowledge of, and experience in, many areas of the curriculum, it presents a unique collection of writings. It should be of interest to subject teachers in schools, to those involved in Initial Teacher Training, as well as to all those acting in advisory capacities or pursuing research.

During 1993, and since the authors of the first book in this series wrote the words quoted above, there has been considerable change nationally in review of the curriculum and assessment, and in processes of school inspection.

Sir Ron Dearing, chairman of the School Curriculum and Assessment Authority, in *The National Curriculum and its Assessment: Interim Report* (1993) has emphasised the crowding of the curriculum and the need to slim down its content. In reference to key stage 2 – 'Since the basic skills must be prescribed in some detail, a significant part of the non-core foundation subjects will need to be translated into non-statutory material for use at the discretion of the teacher'. In reference to key stage 3 the report points to – 'the need to leave scope for teachers to develop opportunities according to the pupils' particular interests and abilities' and, in all key stages, to 'the time released by slimming down the statutorily prescribed content of curriculum would be used to ... teach subjects not included in the National Curriculum, for example, to introduce a foreign language in primary schools, where the teaching skills are available, or to cover issues such as health education and careers education'.

In the OFSTED *Framework for Inspection of Schools*, sections 5.5 and 7.7 describe aspects of the inspection of **spiritual, moral, cultural and social education** and of **equality of opportunity, welfare and guidance**. Work on cross-curricular themes will help schools to provide relevant evidence for inspection of these areas of school life and health education clearly has an important role to play here. Thus, although the cross-curricular themes are not part of the statutory curriculum, which provides the major focus of attention for inspection team members as subject specialists, the total experience of young people in the school is very much influenced by relationships, environment, community links, pupil participation and so on, and these can not be thought of as separate from the ethos of the school. They contribute crucially to spiritual, moral, cultural and social education and to equality of opportunity, welfare and guidance. Health issues are central to all that a school is and does.

National Curriculum Council Guidance

In 1990 the National Curriculum Council for England and Wales published *Curriculum Guidance 5*, to support the introduction of health education in schools. It is clear that many of the elements of health education can be taught through the core and foundation subjects of the National Curriculum, as well as being promoted through many aspects of school life. This curriculum guidance builds on established good practice which in turn had been supported by earlier published advice, some of which still has relevance.

> 'Education for health begins in the home where patterns of behaviour and attitudes influence health for good or ill throughout life and will be established before the child is five. The tasks for schools are to support and promote attitudes, practices and understanding conducive to good health. In so far as they are able to counteract influences which are not conducive to good health, they should do so with sensitive regard to the relationship which exists between children and their families' (DES, 1986, p.1).

Curriculum Guidance 5 provides a framework for school planning and review of current practice. It identifies nine health components or topics: substance use and misuse; sex education; family life education; food and nutrition; safety; health-related exercise; personal hygiene; environmental aspects of health education; psychological aspects of health education.

Embedded in the principles adopted is the notion that to lead a healthy life pupils need to make the right choices and to develop attitudes and values to make these choices. *Curriculum Guidance 5* provides a clear outline of the areas of study in terms of knowledge, skills and attitudes to be acquired by the end of any key stage, but does not prescribe **how the pupils should be taught.** It leaves teachers and health co-ordinators with the task of adopting and promoting appropriate teaching strategies and encouraging active participation by pupils in the classroom; it leaves senior managers in the school to address the 'social ethos' – the aims, attitudes, values and procedures in the school – as well as the overall relationship with the local community, the physical state of the buildings and the school environment.

Meanwhile health crises are widespread, and international, national and local concern about drug abuse, levels of nutrition and sexual health, have resulted in a number of government-sponsored initiatives. Such isolated initiatives, focusing on particular health issues, such as AIDS or contraception, are not uncommon, but a greater challenge is to provide a whole coherent health programme firmly embedded in experience and informed appropriately by tried and tested processes of health education. It has been suggested that health promotion includes health education, disease prevention, the politics of health, and disease management (French, 1990), and that while **health promotion** may involve direct social action and behavioural change, **health education** is a more practical pursuit, with two important goals among young people: raising levels of understanding of disease and illness, and helping them develop the necessary skills to bring about behaviour change. The importance of health education is founded on the premise that in order to lead a healthy life a young person needs to develop attitudes and values to make health choices, and these are part of the preparation necessary for a full, active part in adult society.

Definitions of health vary between nations, and particularly between individuals. Broadly, in this book, we take the definition to be **the capacity to adapt to changes in life leading to physical, social and mental well-being.** Clearly health is influenced by individual personal circumstances and the nature of the community in which one lives. Physical development and deterioration, transitions at school, work-related problems, infections, family circumstances, death and bereavement, as well as numerous other social and economic factors will have particular associations with a young person's state of health and well-being.

There are many reasons why health education has not been given a high priority by many education authorities, headteachers and teachers. Reasons given include the following:

- there are pressures on the curriculum from many sources;
- many teachers consider themselves ill-prepared in what they believe to be 'medical matters' and feel that they are not equipped to teach about health issues;
- pupils may sometimes see health education as moralising or concerned with matters of ill-health remote from their own lives (see Young and Williams, 1989).

This book aims to provide support for teachers of health education in schools. We believe that it is possible to overcome the obstacles mentioned above by using the whole curriculum to acknowledge and deliver aspects of health education.

The scene is set in Chapter 2 for the concept of the 'health promoting school'. Positive action is identified in such a school in a range of ways – the hidden curriculum, identification of agreed social aims and expectations of the school (its ethos), a focus on the quality of the relationships between school and community, acknowledgement of the physical environment through provision of a stimulating and safe place to work and play and an emphasis on healthy eating. Health choices are believed to be made more effectively in such an environment.

The political agenda indicates many tensions, nowhere more clearly stated than in the *Health of the Nation* (Department of Health, 1992). It is for this reason we have included, as Chapter 3, an exploration of this document by a key health professional. We believe school health educators and co-ordinators will find the summary here presented a useful one. Schools do not function in a vacuum but as part of the community. Health care is the subject of much debate, and while its provision is the responsibility of the Department of Health, schools have a crucial role in assisting in the task of improving the health of the nation, and in particular the health of the next generation of young adults and their families. It, therefore, makes sense for the targets of school health education to be informed by wider national health targets.

Chapter 4 addresses cross-curricular skills and their relation to health education. Contributions are from people with considerable experience of in-service work with teachers. The process of health education is crucial to its successful delivery, and successful delivery depends largely on teachers having confidence in a wide range of teaching techniques, rapport with and sensitivity to the needs of young people and having particular skills in being able to handle discussion of controversial issues with openness and dignity. Opportunities are explored for the recording and recognition of achievement in this area.

The contributions to health education by the other four cross-curricular themes (economic and industrial understanding, careers education and guidance, environmental education and education for citizenship) indicate many areas of commonality and complementarity. Contributors with expertise in these areas present their views in Chapter 5.

Sections in Chapter 6 are written by specialists in National Curriculum core and foundation subjects and provide personal views of the many opportunities in the formal curriculum to enhance the provision of health education.

Equality of opportunity is another crucial aspect of effective health education. Contributions to Chapter 7 cover the areas of special needs, gender and multi-cultural issues. These are described, in *Curriculum Guidance 3*, as dimensions of the curriculum, in that entitlement and access for all pupils to the whole curriculum is central to the concept of a National Curriculum. We feel that it is of particular importance, for those involved in health education, to ensure appropriate consideration of the needs of individual pupils with varied abilities, of both sexes and from differing cultures.

Potential links with medical, nursing and dental services are not always fully established or realised by schools. Collaborative work with health professionals, in the school health and psychological services and health promotion services, can be beneficial, and in Chapter 8 some examples of good practice in these areas are described. The involvement of parents and governors in developing a healthy school environment can be invaluable. Finally we include an important section which examines the effect of the media in the arena of health education.

References

Dearing, R. (1993) *The National Curriculum and its Assessment: An Interim Report* London: NCC and SEAC.

Department of Health (1992) *The Health of the Nation* London: HMSO.

DES (1986) *Curriculum Matters 6: Health Education from 5-16* London: HMSO.

Edwards, J. and Fogelman, K. (eds) (1993) *Developing Citizenship in the Curriculum* London: David Fulton Publishers.

Edwards, J. and Pathan, L. (eds) (1993) *Cross-curricular INSET and Resources* Cambridge: Pearson.

French, J. (1990) 'Boundaries and horizons, the role of health education within health promotion', *Health Education Journal*, **49** (1).

Hargreaves, D. (1991) 'Coherence and manageability: reflections on the National Curriculum and cross-curricular provision', *The Curriculum Journal*, **2** (1).

Harrison, J. (1993) *Cross-curricular Themes: Pack 3: Health Education* Cambridge: Pearson.

National Curriculum Council (1992) Working Papers *Setting the scene: commonality in the cross-curricular themes, Overview of the cross-curricular themes* and *Equal opportunities and ERA* York: NCC.

OFSTED (Office for Standards in Education) (1993) *Handbook for the Inspection of Schools* London: HMSO.

Young, I. and Williams, T. (1989) *The Healthy School* Edinburgh: SHEG.

Reference to the following documents occurs repeatedly in the text. They are referred to here in full but will not be so listed as they are mentioned in subsequent pages. Abbreviated references will be given as, for example, **NCC (1990c)** or *Curriculum Guidance 5.*

National Curriculum Council (1990a) *Curriculum Guidance 3: The Whole Curriculum* York: NCC.

National Curriculum Council (1990b) *Curriculum Guidance 4: Economic and Industrial Understanding* York: NCC.

National Curriculum Council (1990c) *Curriculum Guidance 5: Health Education* York: NCC.

National Curriculum Council (1990d) *Curriculum Guidance 6: Careers Education and Guidance* York: NCC.

National Curriculum Council (1990e) *Curriculum Guidance 7: Environmental Education* York: NCC.

National Curriculum Council (1990f) *Curriculum Guidance 8: Education for Citizenship* York: NCC.

CHAPTER 2

Setting the Scene

Jennifer Harrison

What does 'health education' imply?

The meaning of health education has changed slowly over the decades of this century. The practice has shifted its focus from an emphasis on physical health – such as good nourishment and personal hygiene – to a wider agenda embracing mental health and including the skills, sometimes known as life skills, considered necessary for young people. A widening concept together with increasing demand for education in health, have resulted in health education having a more visible profile in schools.

Health as it is defined in the Introduction of this book implies that there is an ultimate state of health to be attained, an ultimate healthy life to be lived and a definitive set of (social) skills to be acquired! The unspoken assumptions underlying health education are numerous. Clearly children and young people are important targets: healthy habits should, it is implicitly argued, be acquired early in life to lay the foundations for health-related behaviours later in life. In spite of this, programmes of health promotion to encourage eating a low fat diet or giving up smoking have, underwritten, a message that **it is never too late** to achieve a healthy lifestyle. In addition some health messages are aimed at a wide spectrum of people, so broadly speaking what is bad for everyone must be bad for you. Indeed it is these behavioural norms that have been encompassed in the targets required of the health promoters.

However, one person's understanding of personal good health may differ very much from another's. If certain unhealthy but controllable behaviours such as smoking, eating junk food and leading a sedentary existence are known to be harmful, why is it that large numbers of people continue to sit around, to smoke and to eat unhealthy food? Traditional explanations have included ignorance of facts, a sense of fatalism, and external forces such as poverty, pace of modern life, or drug addiction. The power of the arguments in *The Nation's Health* (Jacobson, 1988) in addressing in particular, poverty, unemployment and state taxes – which have largely been ignored by subsequent government policy – illustrates such ideological reasoning. Not all will agree with such perspectives, but the statistical evidence of the associations between health and some of these factors makes compelling reading.

The social and the cultural contexts of health education are clearly important factors in determining health behaviour. Research which examined how respondents accounted for life-style at different stages of life (Backett, 1992) suggested that behaviours are regarded as unhealthy only if they are carried out in an inappropriate social context. The adult respondents in two qualitative surveys participated over eighteen months in very free-ranging, semi-structured interviews. Children were viewed as mostly having a healthy life-style, with frequent minor illnesses, but with minimal concern for looking after themselves. Young adults too were viewed as having a classically healthy life-style: they are relatively free of ailments, and unhealthy behaviours such as smoking, drinking and eating junk food are tolerated, partly because they are thought probably not to be permanent, and partly because they are often counterbalanced by an active life. The younger respondents themselves tended to claim that it was boring or middle-aged to worry about life-style, and its implications for illness. Parents as responders, however, claimed greater awareness of their health, and associated life-style, and the social expectation upon them to lead a healthier life. Middle-aged people showed some ambivalence in accepting what might be judged as inevitable or irreversible in terms of life-style or environmental damage, and what might be a more appropriate healthy life-style. The elderly on the other hand generally felt it was pointless to put right a lifetime of bad habits.

If we are to accept that the socio-cultural context is important when developing health practices, it is important to be clear about what exactly the various approaches to health education can achieve. Broadly there are three possible approaches. The first is **disease-orientated** and assumes that each major preventable disease (coronary heart disease, some cancers, Acquired Immune Deficiency Syndrome, and so on) is tackled through a specific programme which is directed at the relevant risk factor. Problems quickly arise as different health professionals may provide conflicting advice, or provide advice in isolation of wider factors. Inevitably the audience is confused and may switch off. If the audience is young people in schools and the health educator is the teacher, each disease is thus approached separately and supported by inconsistent and overlapping advice from health specialists. Nor does such an approach readily fit the curriculum organisation of schools. Even more seriously the approach focusses on the individual's health-related behaviour rather than considering the impact of societal factors on life-style. This view of health is also seriously flawed because it neglects the positive dimensions of health such as well-being and fitness. Tannahill (1990) suggests that such a preventive approach is limited by its very nature:

'Why should people give up valued practices, or adopt new behaviours which they may perceive to be unpleasant, on the strength of some speculative, intangible, preventive benefit? This line of argument is especially applicable to those who have the worst health problems, for whom the present is a grim struggle, whose pleasures are few (and often damaging), and who have little perception of a future worthy of investment or even amenable to personal control.'

The second is another preventive approach which relates to **risk factors.** The aim here is to eliminate the particular risk factors to prevent the disease. It seems to yield fewer problems with duplication since often particular risks are associated with a number of diseases. Nevertheless, such programmes are often expert-dominated, sometimes non-participatory, and again neglect the positive aspects of health. Many health promotion programmes appear to be a mixture of the disease and risk factor approaches.

The third approach is a **health-orientated** one. The priorities of this approach are **places**, with the emphasis in key community settings such as schools, or the workplace or a deprived locality, and **people**, the young or the old, the unemployed or ethnic minority groups. The health needs are determined locally by the deliverers, so the teachers, for example, can be actively involved with initiatives and can tailor them to the needs of the group and the setting. The initiatives are not dropped 'from above' with apparent disregard for the place or the person. An important emphasis in such an approach is that people are involved in defining the health issues, considering the factors affecting the health-related behaviours, and in implementing individual and group action for better health. Citing Tannahill (1990) again:

'Common links in the origins of many types of health-damaging behaviour are recognised – for example, peer and other social pressures (such as those arising out of multiple deprivation) – in relation to the use of alcohol, tobacco and other drugs. In other words a holistic view of health and its determinants prevails.'

The two important aims of such an approach are to enhance positive health, and to prevent ill-health. Health education is, therefore, concerned with the quality of life and the promotion of the physical, social and mental well-being of an individual. It is concerned with the knowledge about what is or is not harmful, and the development of skills to use that knowledge effectively. Leading a healthy life requires young people to make the right choices for themselves. Pupils need to develop attitudes and values to make wise choices both now and in the future. This is a particularly ambitious aim and is one that is shared with social education. Preparing pupils to participate fully, effectively and confidently as responsible adults in society is the ultimate goal.

Problems of curriculum organisation, delivery in the classroom, politics, ethics and morality

(1) Curriculum organisation: health education and the National Curriculum

It is unfortunate, but important to recognise, that there is no shared academic tradition amongst health educators as amongst teachers of English or Geography, who come from a recognised academic and subject-based discipline. Health education in the National Curriculum seems to emerge as an assembly of a wide range of topics – an amalgam of science concepts and associated social and moral concerns. It is worth comparing the nine components in *Curriculum Guidance 5* with the list provided in *The Healthy School* (Young and Williams, 1989, p.13). There are many similarities though the latter includes consumer education and community health care in addition to the nine *Curriculum Guidance 5* health components. The strengths and weaknesses of the topic-based approach demand some reflection. Topic headings do ensure coverage of the curriculum areas, but it is equally important not to lose the more generally pervasive physical, mental and social aspects of health. Indeed this approach has an inherent danger of being fragmented and resulting in a negative, or problem-orientated methodology, which fails to focus on the positive health and well-being of the whole person. The NCC list does take account of the spiral curriculum and the basis of this involves revisiting key areas of health education at intervals in such a way as to develop and expand upon the concepts learned earlier. School-based planning which requires integration into other areas of the curriculum, while at the same time providing progression which relates to the development of the pupils, is a major challenge for a health education co-ordinator. It is also important for teachers to recognise that schools form only part of the influence on a young person's so-called health career. Some influences such as peer pressure are more potent at critical stages of development and prove a stronger influence than teachers or parents at that particular stage. This has to be borne in mind in timing the relevant inputs, for example, in smoking education at school.

Health education is one of the **least** permeated of the cross-curricular themes (Rowe, 1993, p.2). From a school management perspective, health education has a tangible presence, and is more likely than the other cross-curricular themes to have discrete slots in the curriculum, or to be part of a personal and social education programme, or to be associated with a relatively small number of the core and foundation subjects. It is likely to have a written policy, though the existence of this does not necessarily indicate good practice. It is likely to have a designated co-ordinator, backed by an allowance, and to have been supported in recent years by GEST-funded advisory teachers. Health education, therefore, does carry some of the status of an academic school subject.

12

(2) Delivery in the classroom

A widening concept of health education has led to an emphasis in schools on skills, on life skills associated with adolescence, and on enhancement of the quality of life (rather than longevity). The processes used in school programmes of health education are as crucial to the success of the programmes as is the content. Teachers need to provide opportunities for pupils to learn from each other and, importantly, to use language in ways that will influence the organisation of their thoughts. Pupils need a chance to assess evidence and make decisions, to negotiate, to listen, to solve problems, and to make and deal with relationships. They also need the factual input from video tapes and TV programmes, but carefully interleaved with active teaching methodologies. None of these is an easy option for the teacher.

One of the most crucial aspects of the active learning methodology is the development of effective communication skills for discussion of health issues. Schools are required, specifically in the science National Curriculum, to cover the biological facts of sexual reproduction. Indeed it is important to acknowledge and value the presence of this topic in the statutory curriculum. However, the Education Act (1993) has changed the legal requirements in relation to sex education in schools. From August 1994 there will no longer be a statutory requirement within the science National Curriculum to include the study of HIV/AIDS, any other sexually transmitted diseases, or aspects of human sexual behaviour, other than biological aspects. This change has occurred in the face of much opposition, and despite evidence such as that from the National AIDS Trust young people's seminars (National AIDS Trust Youth Initiative, 1991), which indicates that schools may be falling down on providing the chance of effective discussion:

> 'The non-directive discussions appeared to be the method by which the young people felt they learned the most. They wanted the opportunity to be active, believing participation essential for learning. Discussions were considered a good forum for active participation, and through being able to discuss rather than just listen, they would learn more' (p.32).

Clearly the boundaries of confidentiality have to be explored and agreed – these have to be decided by individual schools – and clearly too, pupils cannot be promised that any information they may disclose will not be reported to parents. Nevertheless, the use of secondhand data in the form of case studies, role play, and open-ended problem-solving are all strategies available to teachers or other health professionals. There is no reason why discussion of HIV/AIDS should not take place in, say, English or drama lessons, if this is deemed the most appropriate setting for exploration of the issues.

(3) Political aspects

It is naive to believe that health education can remain politically neutral. In 1976 a publication of the health departments of the UK (DHSS, 1976) indicated that the health of the nation was not exclusively the responsibility of the health professions, and placed a heavy emphasis on the responsibility of individuals for their own health. The emphasis was on the behaviour of individuals rather than on the quality of the environment.

In the intervening years a change of emphasis has taken place. The Secretary of State for Health in the *Health of the Nation* (HMSO, 1992) produced a health strategy for England which identifies key priorities and approaches needed to achieve measurable impact on improving health. This provides political acceptance of the multitude of factors that impinge on the nation's health. It is overt recognition of the environmental and social influences beyond the control of individuals with the quality of life placed high on the political agenda. Action targets have been set for health authorities with five key areas identified: coronary heart disease and stroke, cancers, mental illness, HIV/AIDS and accidents (see Chapter 3).

There are big differences between this list and those found in the WHO *Health for All* targets (WHO, 1985). The latter encompassed broader ideas of equity, community development, environmental protection and better living conditions. Several other reports have acknowledged the part to be played in the state of the nation's health by poverty (rather than ignorance): see the *Black Report* (Black, 1980), *The Health Divide* (Whitehead, 1988) and *The Nation's Health* (Jacobson, 1988). The more recent edition of *The Nation's Health* (Jacobson, 1991) continues to raise questions about necessary political action on state taxes for alcohol and tobacco, drink driving and targeted screening, and to present statistics which illustrate the continuing differing health status between rich and poor in Britain, and the part played by housing, employment, education, transport, and tax policy in the quality of life and health for the poorest citizens of the country.

The government's aims outlined in the *Health of the Nation* (HMSO, 1992) are, according to Iliffe (1991, p.5):

> 'modest and may be difficult to assess. Much of the programme reflects health promotion activities that are already underway, or at least at the active planning stage ... Some of the health problems targeted, like heart disease and stroke, are already changing for the better and further improvements will be difficult to distinguish from the existing trend'.

He raises important questions about just how health authorities will measure the outcomes of their strategies and how health policies can affect other government departments, such as transport and environment.

Curriculum Guidance 3 refers to 'acceptable personal qualities and values' in young people. Just what does this mean? These clearly depend upon

14

gender, economic circumstance and cultural factors among many other things. What does it mean for young people to 'think and act for themselves'? The NCC documentation glosses over the balance between self interest and the constraints which are necessary for co-operative life. There is no reference to wider societal factors such as family structure, cultural context or gender, which in turn may also affect young people's ability to think and act for themselves.

Government intervention in the arena of sex education in schools has been important. In England and Wales responsibility was transferred from local authorities to school governors in the Education Act (No 2) 1986, which provided opportunity for governors of a school to opt a school out of sex education (about 6% did this). More recently in an amendment of the 1993 Education Act, while all secondary schools are now required to provide sex education for their pupils, parents have been given the right to remove their children from sex education lessons. Sex education remains discretionary for primary schools. The 1993 Act through its changes to the statutory science National Curriculum conflicts deeply with Department of Health policy on AIDS education. Current concerns about the rise in teenage conception rates, increase in abortion rates among 15–19 year olds, and trends in sexually transmitted diseases, most notably HIV/AIDS, together with larger social changes which have affected sexuality and liberalisation of attitudes to sex and human relationships, have produced fears in some quarters that sex education leads to unacceptably early sexual experimentation. Research evidence, however, shows little difference in the age of starting to have sexual intercourse among children who have had sex education compared with those who have not (cited in Thomson, 1992, p.24). A whole-school co-ordinated approach to sex education, together with the provision of accessible services, is vital to the long term sexual health of young people.

Drugs education is another area of political concern. The use of illegal drugs is determined by individual, social and international factors, and not especially confined to a particular life-style or socio-economic group. Nevertheless, those most at risk are within a young, but changing group. A growing body of evidence does, however, indicate a link between heroin use and social deprivation. The most useful drug education campaigns for young people are now thought to be those which put legal and illegal drugs into a realistic social and cultural context, and attempt to encourage young people to develop sufficient knowledge and self confidence to make appropriate decisions concerning their use. Educational initiatives have been twofold – to reduce experimentation and to provide treatment and support for those who wish to stop using drugs. Worryingly, some time ago, the Advisory Council on the Misuse of Drugs (ACMD, 1984) concluded that knowledge about drugs can be increased but changes in attitudes are harder to achieve; that sometimes drug education programmes can even be counter-productive, and that mass media campaigns that focus on single drugs and rely on shock tactics are inappropriate. Despite such evidence the mass media campaigns have continued, while longer term initiatives prepared by The Advisory Council on Alcohol and Drug Education and the Institute for the Study of Drug Dependence (TACADE/ISDD, 1986) provide low key approaches in line with the latest ACMD recommendations (ACMD, 1993).

(4) Ethical and moral aspects

Curriculum Guidance 5 suggests a wide range of topics (components). In order to establish some coherence and pay attention to ethical and moral issues, it would be helpful for teachers working collaboratively to define what might be 'a healthy life-style' for young people. More than this, teachers will also have to pay attention to what it means to be a person and to develop as a person. Hargreaves (1982) wrote in *The Challenge for the Comprehensive School:*

> 'Our present secondary school system, largely through the hidden curriculum, exerts on many pupils, particularly but by no means exclusively from the working class, a destruction of their dignity which is so massive and pervasive that few subsequently recover from it.'

During their health careers people become aware of the external influences on personal decision-making and ultimately of choice over health-related issues. In taking stock of their own position on a social and moral issue such as contraception or abortion they need time to compare values and beliefs held by themselves and others in order to find the common ground, and to consider the moral dilemma, both personal and social. Informed decision-making needs also to take account of the difficulty that the difference between right and wrong is not always straightforward. Respect for different ways of living, beliefs and opinions permeates much of the work done in health education, so illuminating for instance the meaning of 'relationships' within families, between friends and within communities. In the formal curriculum there is an important link to be made in using factual health-related knowledge in decision-making settings. Indeed topics such as drug abuse, family planning and contraception cannot be taught in a moral vacuum.

There are clear links, therefore, with ethical education and moral education. Health education has to encompass the debate about 'right' and 'wrong' over issues to do with drugs, sex education, contraception, abortion and so on. This raises the question about what are the criteria for 'good' and 'bad'? How can any personal decision-making take place without recognisable criteria? For example, in promoting life enhancement, teachers have to address aspects of social health. Are we really all the same? Do we all really have to acquire the same life skills which accompany health? It falls within the role of teachers of literature or religion or humanities to enrich the moral tradition so a young person can come to a decision over these issues. Indeed without any moral tradition it is difficult for a young person to come to his or her own decision.

Conclusion

Planning for health education and health promotion is subject to much scrutiny and debate in the UK. Two recent reports, one from the Health Education Board for Scotland (SHEG, 1990) and the other from the Scottish Home and Health Department (SHHD, 1990), indicate the need for a holistic approach to health education rather than separate programmes and advocate the 'positive life-styles approach' within a broader context of health promotion. This is clearly at odds with the current delivery and emphasis in the UK through single preventive topics, for example, on issues related to coronary heart disease.

Health education as seen within the larger concept of health promotion indicates the need to integrate health education planning with the other facets of health promotion. In order to engage with health education planning, which utilises the holistic, health-orientated approach, teachers as health educators, need to:

(1) have an awareness of the significance of disease and risk factors;
(2) respond to new threats to health such as AIDS;
(3) promote the uptake of screening services and immunisation programmes;
(4) use any opportunities to promote health issues;
(5) meet special needs of pupils who have been identified in 'high' or 'at risk' groups;
(6) put into place policies which ensure health protection such as 'No Smoking' and 'Healthy Eating';
(7) respond to specific needs as identified by individuals and the community.

What should emerge is a co-ordinated programme which can take account of the local health promotion strategies and is strengthened by good lines of communication with local public health and health promotion officers. Health education has a central role in providing high quality health information, which includes the social and economic determinants of health. It has a role also in developing people's ability to understand and take control of their health status – an ability which is clearly based on development of appropriate skills in order to bring about change.

Health education is not about behaviour change, nor is it overt political action. By allowing people to set their own health agenda, health education has the opportunity to promote self-esteem, to use voluntary initiatives rather than be rooted in propaganda, to respect cultural differences as well as other social and economic constraints, to avoid stereotyping and prejudice, and critically to examine health information and how it is used. Health messages are necessarily complex, and the potential negative effects of any programme should always be examined carefully.

Seedhouse (1986) has likened the process of health education to the building of the foundations of a good building. Using this analogy health education can be seen as the means of enabling young people to achieve their chosen health goals. The building process should cease at that point. Perhaps the best health education can do is to allow young people to face questions of health directly and to think for themselves.

In summary, the role of teachers as health educators in school, is to place issues that are so often pushed off to the health professional (the doctor, the dentist, the nutritionist) firmly into the school and its community. If young people have a grasp on the health information and the surrounding issues, together with a mastery of the language, they are much more likely to be in control of their own health choices.

Finding a way to achieve a common approach in schools

The Health Promoting School

The European Symposium (Peebles, Scotland, May 1986) which was a joint venture of World Health Organisation (WHO European Office) and the Scottish Health Education Group (SHEG) had as a context the document *Targets for Health for All* (WHO, 1985). In this was an acknowledgement of the fundamental requirements for people to be healthy and a set of proposals for action to secure improvements in these conditions. A major principle was that inequity in health can and must be reduced, and that people must be given social and economic opportunities to develop and maintain their health.

In particular the conference addressed targets 15 and 16:

'by 1990, educational programmes in all member states should enhance the knowledge, motivation and skill of people to organise and maintain health';

'by 1995, in all member states, there should be significant increase in positive health behaviour, such as balanced nutrition, non-smoking, appropriate physical activity and good stress management'.

The term 'Health Promoting School' was coined at the Peebles conference and it has become a unifying concept because it provides **an important point of reference** for the differing perceptions of school health education held by teachers, doctors, nurses, parents, administrators and social workers. It also links strongly with the notion of health promotion developed in *Health Promotion: A Discussion Document on the Concept and Principles* (WHO, 1984):

'... health promotion ... has come to represent a unifying concept for those who recognise the need for change in the ways and conditions of living, in order to promote health ... represents a **mediating strategy between people and their environment**, synthesising personal choices and social responsibilities in health to create a healthier future'.

The school environments

In schools there are many different environments – intellectual, spiritual, social, psychological and cultural – within which pupils both work and play, and which influence the way pupils learn, think and behave.

'... it behoves the caring educator to enquire whether its **(the school's)** general ambience is, at the least, supportive of the health and well-being of its pupils and, at best, actively promoting their healthy life-styles' (SHEG/WHO, 1986).

Such an approach involves teachers not only in the taught course, but in the demonstration by the school that health is important. Using the WHO terminology the school must become 'health promoting'. Influences such as the nature of the food served in the dining area, the state of cleanliness of the cloakrooms and toilets, the presence of litter bins, and a stimulating, safe environment, are largely 'unseen' but powerful messages. In their presence it is clear that the healthy choices appear to be the easier choices.

Fundamental to the health promoting school is the hidden curriculum which includes the caring relationships developed between home and school and the physical environment and facilities of the school.

'Pupils notice the courtesies, concern, tolerance, negotiation and general care taken of the environment. They notice the behaviour of adults in, for example, contradictory attitudes to smoking in playground and staffroom. The subtle messages communicated by teachers' behaviour to pupils have profound effects on what pupils learn' (SHEG, 1990, pp.16–17).

A health promoting school starts with the **pupils** – a close examination of pupils' present knowledge, attitudes and needs is important, but not enough. Pupils should be consulted about their perceived needs, for example, in areas like sex education (RCOG, 1991). The reasons for young people taking up habits and behaving in ways which are harmful to their health are numerous and complex. Seeking experiences beyond the ordinary, or taking risks which make the pupils feel good, provide a challenge to schools to provide a choice of stimulating opportunities to pupils – for example, in music, drama, residential work, field trips and outdoor education in general.

For health education in its widest sense the processes and experiences of learning are just as important as the content. Developing skills of building good relationships, and strategies for dealing with peer pressure, are important elements of the social environment of the school. Pupils are more likely to think positively about health matters and to modify behaviour which is potentially harmful if they have a sense of their own self worth. Schools have to exploit every opportunity to allow pupils to practise taking responsibility for their actions and the consequences.

Equally important are the teachers themselves: teachers who are not severely stressed, overworked and undervalued are an essential part of the health promoting school. Providing opportunities for their choices and decisions also reflects the healthy social environment of the school.

The geographic area served by schools seldom represents a single community with common views and interests. It is likely to consist of groups holding different attitudes to school and having different expectations of it. Particular health issues will have different significance to different groups and, therefore, their importance cannot be assumed. To establish the views of the parents is important, and this is particularly vital in sensitive areas such as sex education. There is a shared responsibility which acknowledges children's experiences at home, most particularly in areas such as attitudes to eating, smoking, drinking and sex. Finding opportunities for discussion with parents and for sharing the approaches used by the school is paramount to the success of a school health education programme. Parents often do not realise the important educational role they play themselves. Schools have an important part to play in maintaining regular contact with the home.

'Actual involvement in the curriculum and in children's learning remains controversial but the development of a meaningful two-way curriculum discussion depends upon schools regarding parents as partners in the education of their children' (Young and Williams, 1989).

The **community** is defined as the environment surrounding the school, leisure facilities, welfare services, meeting points, libraries – in fact all the social and physical fabric upon which the community depends. Acknowledgement by the health promoting school of the health and caring services in providing health screening and immunisation and the role played by the psychological and social work services is important. Community and environmental projects in a true community school can be of benefit to all participants. Active co-operation can be found, for example, in community service placements for pupils, and in welcoming and mixing with adults in class and community groups.

Establishing a network of health promoting schools

What has been the progress since 1986? A collaborative project involving WHO (European Office), the Commission of the European Community

(CEC) and the Council of Europe (CE) is to establish a European network of health promoting schools, with the aim of achieving healthy life-styles for the total school population, by developing supportive environments conducive to the promotion of health. The development builds on the report of Young and Williams (1989) which:

> '... emphasises that the whole life and environment of a school can become a health promoting force. Such schools will have a planned curriculum which will allow learning related to major health issues such as AIDS to occur in a meaningful context which relates to all the health needs of young people'.

It offers opportunities for, and requires commitment to, the provision of a safe and health-enhancing social and physical environment. It should result in the exchange of experiences, information, and the dissemination of good practice.

The selection of the schools depends upon their willingness to meet a number of criteria which are summarised below:

- active promotion of the self-esteem of all pupils by demonstrating that everyone can make a contribution to the life of the school;
- the development of good relations between staff and pupils and between pupils in the daily life of the school;
- the clarification for staff and pupils of the social aims of the school;
- the provision of stimulating challenges for all pupils through a wide range of activities;
- using every opportunity to improve the physical environment of the school;
- the development of good links between the school, the home and the community;
- the development of good links between associated primary and secondary schools to plan a coherent health education curriculum;
- the active promotion of the health and well-being of the staff;
- the consideration of the role of staff exemplars in health-related issues;
- the consideration of the role of school meals (if provided) to the health education curriculum;
- the realisation of the potential of specialist services in the community for advice and support in health education;
- the development of the education potential of the school health services beyond routine screening towards active support for the curriculum.

At the time of writing the UK will be included in the list of member states of the European network of schools (September, 1993) bringing the total to 37 participating members. It is an exciting project, which makes enormous strides to address at least some of the problems of teaching and learning in the arena of health education in school.

With an approach that is clearly placing an emphasis on relationships, and endeavouring to raise institutional awareness of these as an important factor in the success of health education, and with a curriculum of common themes that is by no means prescriptive, the project goes well beyond the individualistic model of health education in *Curriculum Guidance 5*. The project provides a shift from an emphasis on individual understanding, self-knowledge and personal responsibility to an emphasis on the wider structures of the health promoting community. Research findings and experience gained by the work of the CE, WHO and CEC indicate the importance of using a single but effective project concept:

> 'the concerns, interests and energies of everyone in the school setting are mobilised to identify and use opportunities for health ... it helps schools to be accepted as focal points for health promotion initiatives in their communities' (European Network of Health Promoting Schools, 1993, section 1.4).

It is believed that only in this way can health education be truly successful for individual pupils.

References

Advisory Council for the Misuse of Drugs (ACMD) (1984) *Prevention – A Report* London: HMSO.

ACMD (1993) *Drug Education in Schools – A Need for a New Impetus* London: HMSO.

Backett, K. and Davison, C. (1992) 'Rational or reasonable? Perceptions of health at different stages of life', *Health Education Journal*, **51** (2), 55–59.

Black, D. (1980) *Inequalities in Health: Report of a Research Working Group* London: DHSS.

Department of Health and Social Security (DHSS) (1976) *Prevention and Health: Everybody's Business* London: HMSO.

European Network of Health Promoting Schools (ENHPS) (1993) Extracts from the *Resource Manual for Use by National Co-ordinators* Copenhagen: WHO Regional Office.

Hargreaves, D. (1982) *The Challenge for the Comprehensive School* London: Routledge and Kegan Paul.

HMSO (1992) *The Health of the Nation. A Strategy for Health in England* London: HMSO.

Iliffe, S. (1991) 'More questions than answers', *Health Matters,* Issue 8.

Jacobson, B. (ed) (1988) *The Nation's Health: A Strategy for the 1990s* King Edward's Hospital Fund for London.

Jacobson, B. (ed) (1991) *The Nation's Health* (revised edition) King Edward's Hospital Fund for London.

National AIDS Trust Youth Initiative (1991) *Living for Tomorrow* London: The National AIDS Trust.

Rowe, G., Aggleton, P. and Whitty, G. (1993) *Subjects and themes in the School Curriculum* (Working paper for ESRC project *Assessing Quality in Cross Curricular Context*) University of London, Institute of Education.

RCOG (Royal College of Obstetricians and Gynaecologists) (1991) *Report of RCOG Working Party on Unplanned Pregnancy* London: RCOG.

SHEG/WHO (Scottish Health Education Group/World Health Organisation) (1986) *The Health Promoting School: Report of the European Symposium, Peebles* WHO, European Office, and SHEG, Edinburgh.

SHEG (1990) *Promoting Good Health: Proposals for Action in Schools* Edinburgh: SHEG.

SHHD (Scottish Home and Health Department) (1990) *A Review of Health Education in Scotland* Edinburgh: SHHD.

Seedhouse, D. (1986) *Health: The Foundations for Achievement* Chichester: Wiley.

TACADE/ISDD (1986) *Drugwise* London: TACADE.

Tannahill, A. (1990) 'Health education and health promotion: planning for the 1990s', *Health Education Journal,* **49** (4) 194–198.

Thomson, R. and Scott, L. (1992) *An Enquiry into Sex Education* London: National Children's Bureau Sex Education Forum.

Whitehead, M. (1992) 'The health divide' in Townsend, P. and Davidson, N. (eds) (1992), *Inequalities in Health* London: Penguin.

WHO (1985) *Targets for Health for All by the Year 2000* Copenhagen: WHO Regional Office.

WHO (1984) *Health Promotion: A Discussion Document on the Concept and Principles* Copenhagen: WHO.

Young, I. and Williams, T. (1989) *The Healthy School* Edinburgh: SHEG.

Details of the **Health Promoting School Network** can be obtained from the International Planning Committee, c/o Health Promotion Unit, WHO Regional Office for Europe, Scherfigsvej 8, DK-2100 Copenhagen, Denmark (Tel (+45) 39 17 15 76).

The Scottish Health Education Group (SHEG) is now known as the **Health Education Board for Scotland** (HEBS), and the address is: Woodburn House, Canaan Lane, Edinburgh EH10 4SG; (tel 031-447-8044).

CHAPTER 3

The Health of the Nation: A Strategic Framework

Gillian Morgan

Introduction

The World Health Organisation (WHO) defines health as 'a state of complete physical, mental and social well-being and not merely the absence of disease or infirmity'. This complex definition emphasises the positive aspects of health that go far beyond the physical status and longevity of individuals. Improvement in the health status of populations or individuals requires a complex range of societal interventions. Most are beyond the scope of health services alone. The definition underpins the Declaration of Alma Ata (1978) which set a goal of 'Health For All by the Year 2000'. The UK government was amongst the signatories committed to 'protect and promote the health of all the people of the world'. In 1985 the European Region of the WHO translated the declaration into 38 targets (WHO, 1985; O'Neill, 1983). These range from the reduction of inequalities in health experience between different socio-economic groups within countries, to the eradication of specific infectious diseases through immunisation. Writing in 1993, it is ironic that a target to improve health by the eradication of war was not included as it was felt to be irrelevant to Europe in the late twentieth century. The targets include some numerical standards but many are merely general statements. This makes assessment of success subjective. Currently the UK has clearly achieved eight targets, has failed to reach eight targets and has made some progress on the remainder. The degree of success in this latter category is unclear and dependent on subjective assessment. The declaration also committed signatories to the development of national health strategies. The UK achieved this by the publication of *The Health of the Nation* (Department of Health, 1992).

Preventing Disease

The potential of preventive strategies to improve health underpins *The Health of the Nation*. Prevention is normally described as having three levels (Donaldson, 1983). **Primary prevention** involves strategies aimed at preventing the onset of disease. Successful programmes include immunisation against smallpox, eradicated world-wide, and, in the UK, immunisation against other infectious diseases including diphtheria and polio which are virtually eradicated in this country. Primary prevention programmes that aim to reduce disease by encouraging behaviour change are, however, generally less successful. Just under a third of adults still smoke, despite thirty years of publicity about the dangers of smoking and widespread public knowledge about the potential risks. Even more alarming is the recent increase in smoking amongst adolescents, particularly girls, despite health promotional campaigns and the inclusion of health educational programmes within the school curricula. For many diseases, the most appropriate design of a primary preventive strategy is unclear as the causation of the disease must be understood and intervention possible. This difficulty is heightened as many of the common diseases of the late twentieth century are multifactorial, ie they have multiple causes, many of which are not amenable to change and some of which appear to have opposing effects on other diseases. The scientific evidence for some suggested changes is complex and confusing and the public are frequently bombarded with conflicting and contradictory messages. There are also ethical dilemmas. Should efforts be concentrated on the small number of individuals at high risk, each of whom will receive a significant personal health benefit by making the recommended life-style change or on a programme aimed at the entire population, each individual only gaining a small personal benefit but required, nevertheless, to make a significant change in behaviour? The paradox and difficulty is created as the former approach, whilst beneficial to the individuals involved, will save fewer lives than the broader population approach. There is no right answer to this conundrum and advocates of both approaches can be identified.

Much primary prevention involves educational interventions that aim to increase knowledge about more healthy life-styles. Success is frequently measured by changes in knowledge and attitudes rather than changes in behaviour and health status. In part this reflects the long time it takes to demonstrate changes in health status whilst increased knowledge can easily be demonstrated immediately. It is believed that increased knowledge and a change in attitude about a life-style factor will lead to a change in behaviour, and, eventually to a change in health outcome. This is over-simplistic as it is clear that, for many behaviours, there is a high level of knowledge about the most healthy life-styles within the population. For example, there is a very high level of knowledge about the adverse effects of smoking amongst smokers, including adolescents. Indeed a high proportion of smokers have negative attitudes towards smoking, nearly 7 in 10 supporting banning smoking in public places and 6 in 10 banning tobacco advertising (NOP, 1987, 1988, 1989). Over half of those classifying themselves as regular smokers would like to give up and have tried to do so but have failed. Knowledge and attitudes are thus, in themselves, ineffective in stimulating behaviour change. It has been demonstrated, however, that the single most effective measure to reduce smoking, would be the increase in the price of tobacco; it has been estimated that a 1% increase would reduce smoking by 0.5% and vice versa (Townsend, 1992). This simple fiscal intervention would, however, require governmental commitment which is currently lacking; the price of cigarettes declined in real terms between 1986 and 1993.

A further complication is that knowledge of a healthier life-style cannot generate a change in behaviour if the means of making the change is not accessible. For example, there is now a high level of knowledge about the composition of a healthy diet. The components of this diet, for example, fresh fruit, lean meat and whole-wheat bread are more expensive than their less beneficial alternatives and many people cannot, therefore, afford to live healthily. Similarly the stimulation of increased knowledge and positive attitudes about condom use as part of a preventive strategy to reduce sexually transmitted diseases and pregnancy, will be ineffective unless individuals have ready access to condoms when required. Finally it is clear that preventive programmes can be highly successful without generating knowledge and attitudinal change. The impact of seat belt legislation for car users and crash helmet legislation for motor bike riders has been significant in reducing fatal injuries. Both were opposed by a significant minority but once they became law, compliance has been high. These examples demonstrate a broader approach to changing behaviour. This approach, which focusses on positive aspects of health and not merely disease avoidance and encompasses legal, fiscal, environmental, occupational and societal interventions in addition to educational strategies, has come to be called 'health promotion'. Whilst health services have some responsibilities in these areas many other groups have already made significant contributions in this area and have the potential to make greater changes than the health services. The education service is amongst the key players.

Secondary prevention involves the detection of disease at an early stage to allow effective treatment and, where possible, cure. Screening whole populations for disease before any symptoms are present is one variant of this approach. Screening is used for some form of cancers, particularly cervical and breast cancer, for high blood pressure, during ante-natal care and during childhood health surveillance programmes. It is a very expensive approach and its success depends on a high uptake by the population. Whilst secondary prevention is clearly the area where health services have the major responsibility other services can contribute greatly, particularly in encouraging appropriate and effective use of services thus ensuring that individuals are informed consumers of health care.

Tertiary prevention includes rehabilitation or care where a disease process is irreversible. Rehabilitation aims to help individuals reach and maintain their maximum functional capacity. Health services again have some role to play but other agencies, the voluntary sector and, most significantly individuals themselves, their family and friends make an even greater contribution. Within the educational setting teachers may be involved with children with special needs. Special programmes for these children, whether educational or physical, help to make these children healthier, within the WHO definition discussed earlier. Increasingly this type of programme is delivered within the community. Family and other carers are providing increasing amounts of the required support. Children are involved in providing care and recent reports have highlighted the pressure on children, some as young as six, who act as primary carers for parents (Aldridge, 1993). Many of these children report concern that they will be separated from the parent and, therefore, shoulder significant burdens without asking for help. Teachers will need to be sensitive to this issue as community care increases.

Health of the Nation

For some years there has been considerable interest in the prevention of disease. The first government publication on the issue, *Prevention and Health: Everybody's Business* (HMSO, 1976) was launched by Barbara Castle, then Secretary of State for Social Services. This document responded to concerns about escalating health care costs, the increase of incurable, chronic diseases, for example, coronary heart disease and cancers rather than acute illness; and the relatively poor health status of the UK population when compared with the population of similar countries. More recently this belief in prevention underpinned *Promoting Better Health* (DHSS, 1987), the first of three major White Papers on Health Services issued during the late 1980s. This increased the emphasis on prevention within the routine activities of General Practice. GPs are set targets for immunisation and cervical cytology screening rates and are paid a bonus for achievement. Health screens carried out on new patients and on older (over 75) patients are also included within contractual requirements. GPs can be further remunerated for running health promotion clinics aimed at helping people live healthier lives and at reducing some of the major risk factors for disease.

The Health of the Nation is the most recent central initiative. Published in July 1992 it is the first strategy for health adopted by the Department of Health. It differs from preceding documents as, instead of an all-encompassing approach to health, five programme areas are identified for action. Within these areas twenty-five long term targets are set for achievement between 1995 and 2005. Health authorities are monitored on progress towards these targets and on a number of shorter term, interim measures. Hitherto target setting for the National Health Service has concentrated on short term (one or two year) achievement of simpler, activity measures, for example, the numbers of people on waiting lists or the maximum waiting time for admission. In strategic development the English health service lags somewhat behind the Welsh Office which published its own ambitious document *Strategic Intent and Direction For The NHS In Wales* (Welsh Health Planning Forum, 1989). This influential document has gone further in many respects, attempting to meld the health promotion and disease prevention agenda with the task of delivering effective efficient and responsive health services. It also publicised the concept of 'Health Gain'; adding life to years as well as years to life.

The Health of the Nation was preceded by the publication of a consultation document that discussed a range of possible approaches to improving health. A large number of comments was received from health authorities and health professionals and, equally importantly from local authorities, education departments, voluntary groups and interested individuals. Three broad approaches were advocated. Firstly, a medical model using disease categories selected because of the numbers of people dying or affected by the condition, the severity of the condition, its impact on those affected and the scope for prevention. Secondly, a life-style model, focusing on behaviours known to cause illness and thus produce improvements in health by stimulating behaviour change. For example, a reduction in smoking in the population would decrease a wide range of diseases including coronary heart disease, cancers of the lung, mouth, throat and cervix as well as reducing the numbers of low birth weight babies born, the numbers of babies dying from sudden infant death syndrome (cot death) and the numbers of children developing asthma. The third approach, particularly advocated by local authorities, is societal, trying to improve health by looking at the broader determinants of health and well-being including poverty, deprivation, poor housing and the environment.

The consultation also considered the number of areas to be selected for action, irrespective of the approach chosen. Whilst many respondents expressed concern about the impact of selecting only a few areas, on areas not selected the majority view was that a limited number of issues should be prioritised nationally leaving scope for further action at a local area when other issues were deemed to be more or equally important. There was, however, as would be expected, less agreement about which areas should be selected with many pressure groups arguing cogently and forcibly why their particular issue should be given priority.

Finally the use of targets was discussed. The use of numerical targets has certain benefits. They can highlight important areas, assist in converting programmes to policies and focus managerial action on key areas. If numerical they allow progress to be measured, introducing accountability and discipline in policy makers and target setters. The development of targets requires the collection of good data and a logical approach to the analysis of this information to clarify the best programme of action. The approach also has drawbacks; it can lead to an inappropriate focus on the measurable rather than the important and a neglect of other issues. Numerical targets can become an over-simplistic description of a complex policy. Targets must be realistic; over-ambitious targets can result in a lack of real effort as achievement is felt to be impossible; if too simple then complacency can be generated. In addition targets must be reviewed and revised regularly to ensure they remain relevant and responsive to changes in treatments.

Following the consultation the Department of Health chose to adopt a medical model for the strategy, focusing on five disease areas and using a target-setting approach. Health authorities are, however, encouraged to develop local health strategies to complement the national document and make it more relevant to the special needs of local communities. This can involve inclusion of additional priorities or the development of local or shorter term versions of the twenty-five national targets. Health authorities are held accountable for achievement of these national and local targets through the formal managerial chain. Thus for the first time since the inception of the NHS in 1948 managers are being held responsible for improving the long term health of the population they serve. This is even more remarkable as the majority of interventions, required to achieve the targets, lie outside the control of health services and most lie beyond the normally short, managerial, ministerial and governmental time frame.

The *Health of the Nation* recognises that health cannot be improved by health services alone and requires the active co-operation and participation of a wide range of organisations and individuals. To demonstrate that this commitment is more than rhetoric, the cabinet established a committee on health with Tony Newton as chair. This brings together ministers from key governmental departments. The commitment is applauded, however, it must be noted that the impact expected from this high level group has yet to be felt and individual departmental policies continue to be inconsistent and at times even contradictory. Within the education sector this is most clearly demonstrated by the withdrawal of Grants for Education and Support Training (GEST) funding for health education posts and resources, concurrently with the launch and implementation of the *Health of the Nation* with its focus on promoting health in young people. The Secretary of State for Education (1993) chose to focus this funding on reducing truancy and on inner city initiatives. One could argue about the potential of these investments for improving education and health, nevertheless, it demonstrates an inconsistency in approach.

The final document, with its adoption of a medical model, has been criticised because of the lack of comment about the broader determinants of health and in particular the neglect of poverty and deprivation and the effect of these on health. Inequalities in the health status of different socio-economic groups remain marked in the UK. A boy born to a social class 5 mother is one and a half times more likely to die by the age of 15 than one born to a social class 1 mother. Deaths from accidents, poisoning and respiratory disease are particularly increased. Children in single parent families are even more vulnerable with three times the death rate of social class 1 children. This sector of the population is one of the most rapidly increasing in society and it is estimated that 1 million children are now included (Judge, 1993). *Inequalities in Health* (Black, 1980) and *The Health Divide* (Whitehead, 1992) discuss the social class differences observed in the UK and the possible explanations for these. It is regrettable that inequalities have increased rather than decreased over recent years.

Components of Health of the Nation

The *Health of the Nation* focusses on five key areas: coronary heart disease and stroke; cancers; accidents; sexual health; and mental health.

(1) Coronary heart disease (CHD) and stroke

CHD AND STROKE TARGETS

1. *To reduce death rates for both coronary heart disease and stroke in people under 65 by at least 40% by the year 2000.*
2. *To reduce the death rate from CHD in people aged 65–74 by at least 30% by the year 2000.*
3. *To reduce the death rate from stroke in people aged 65–74 by at least 40% by the year 2000.*

Coronary heart disease is caused by a narrowing or blockage in the arteries supplying blood to the heart. This can result in pain during exercise (angina), a heart attack caused by an acute blockage or even sudden death. It causes more than one in four of all deaths and is the single most common cause of premature death. Treatment of those affected uses one fortieth of all the resources invested in the NHS. Thirty-five million working days are lost because of the disease. Stroke causes one in eight of all deaths and is also a major cause of disability, particularly in older people. Treatment and care of those affected uses one seventeenth of all NHS resources. About 7.7 million working days are lost due to the condition.

The main factors associated with an increased risk of these conditions are cigarette smoking, raised blood cholesterol levels, high blood pressure and low levels of physical exercise. All of these factors can be influenced by changes in behaviour. The single most important factor is cigarette smoking which has also been linked to a number of other conditions as discussed above. The risks of smoking have been clearly demonstrated in a large number of scientific studies. Risk is increased in heavy smokers and in those who have been smoking for the longest periods. Whilst publicity led to a decline in smoking this has slowed over recent years and smoking has actually increased in young women. Children are more likely to smoke if their parents and siblings do so but there is also evidence of a peer group effect. The *Health of the Nation* has set an ambitious interim target for the reduction of smoking in children by at least 33% by 1994. This already seems doomed to failure; health authorities alone cannot reach young people effectively and recent changes within the educational sector have made co-ordination of programmes much more difficult. The problem is also compounded by the conflicting messages from central government. The UK is unwilling to endorse a ban on cigarette advertising, despite its own report demonstrating a reduction in consumption of between 4 and 8% in countries which have done so (Department of Health, 1993; Health Education Authority, 1993). The ambiguities are even more profound; the EEC currently invests about £7 million per year in cancer prevention campaigns, much of this is directed against smoking. In parallel, however, the community invests £900 million per year in subsidising tobacco farmers through the Common Agricultural Policy (CAP). Indeed this makes tobacco the most highly subsidised of all crops within the CAP receiving £1700 per minute in subsidies, 2.3% of the total budget of the community (Miller, 1993).

On a smaller scale there are discrepancies in the approaches to smoking adopted locally. Schools teach the dangers of smoking from an early age yet very few have comprehensive smoking policies which embrace the teaching staff as well as pupils. How can children be expected to take messages seriously when they walk past smoke drifting from under the staff room door? Far too many councils still allow councillors to smoke during meetings and the majority fail to make use of their legal powers, for example, to prosecute shops selling cigarettes to under age children. Some impressive sports events continue to be supported by tobacco companies which create an image of health around the sale of the most damaging chemical available legally. Voluntary agreements are inadequate; tobacco companies need to recruit 300 new smokers a day merely to replace those who die. Preventing children becoming smokers or reducing the numbers who become heavy smokers must be a cornerstone of any strategy to improve our nation's health.

SMOKING TARGETS

4. *To reduce the prevalence of cigarette smoking to no more than 20% by the year 2000 in both men and women (a reduction of a third).*
5. *To reduce consumption of cigarettes by at least 40% by the year 2000.*
6. *In addition to the overall reduction in prevalence, at least a third of women smokers to stop smoking at the start of their pregnancy by the year 2000.*
7. *To reduce smoking prevalence in 11–15 year olds by at least a third by 1994, to less than 6%.*

A high level of blood cholesterol is associated with increased mortality from CHD. Although there is continuing debate about the most effective way of reducing these levels it is clear that those who consume a high proportion of saturated fats found in meat products and those who are obese are most likely to have high levels. Specific targets have, therefore, been set on both these issues. Overweight and obesity are associated with reduced exercise as well as excess food and calorie consumption. Preventive strategies, therefore, include the encouragement of a healthy diet with limited red meat, plenty of fruit and vegetables and fibre from cereals. Schools can contribute to this process by teaching and by example; recent surveys of school meals have suggested that the nutritional content could easily be improved if schools regarded meals as a core component of a health strategy. Schools are also well placed to encourage patterns of exercise that can be carried on into adult life. Recent years have seen a decline in the numbers of people who continue to participate in sport once they leave school; perhaps the form of exercise encouraged at school is not felt to be fun or worth continuation? Alcohol use is associated with obesity and with increased blood pressure. In addition it is a significant contributor to accident deaths, particularly in young men.

Alcohol abuse is also extremely damaging socially. The levels of alcohol use in young people are increasing; it is clear that its use is accepted as the norm rather than the exception. Strategies need to empower young people to help them resist peer pressure; this is best taught as part of a comprehensive programme.

DIET AND NUTRITION

8. *To reduce the average percentage of food energy derived by the population from saturated fatty acids by at least 35% by 2005.*
9. *To reduce the average percentage of food energy derived from total fat by the population by at least 12% by 2005.*
10. *To reduce the proportion of men and women aged 16–64 who are obese by at least 25% and 33% respectively by 2005.*
11. *To reduce the proportion of men drinking more than 21 units of alcohol per week and women drinking more than 14 units per week by 30% by 2005.*

HYPERTENSION

12. *To reduce mean systolic blood pressure in the adult population by at least 5mm Hg by 2005.*

Obesity is also associated with increased blood pressure levels, a major predictor of risk of stroke. Increased blood pressure is uncommon in young people but factors which influence its onset are common. Intervention at this stage could significantly reduce subsequent problems.

(2) Cancers

Cancers are the second most common cause of death in the UK. The view of cancer as a universally fatal condition is a myth; there are many different types of cancer with differing prognoses. Many are preventable if more healthy life-styles are adopted whilst others can be detected at an early stage and cured. Four cancers have been selected for especial attention because of the potential for reducing death by changing behaviour or ensuring better coverage of screening programmes. Overall the single most important cause of cancer is smoking which is estimated to be the cause of at least 30% of all deaths from cancer in addition to its major contribution to cardiovascular disease.

CANCER TARGETS

13. To reduce the death rate for lung cancer by at least 30% in men under 75 and 15% in women under 75 by 2010.

14. To reduce the death rate for breast cancer in the population invited for screening by at least 25% by the year 2000.

15. To reduce the incidence of invasive cervical cancer by at least 20% by the year 2000.

16. To halt the year on year increase in the incidence of skin cancer by 2005.

LUNG CANCER

This is the single most common cause of death from cancer. At least 8 of every 10 deaths from the disease are smoking related, either directly or through passive smoking. Many of the issues related to smoking are discussed above as is the most important objective of stopping children starting to smoke in the first place. The importance of this and the central role of the education sector cannot be over-emphasised. Prevention is the only way of reducing premature deaths as treatment is ineffective and there has been no improvement in survival over the past 20 years. Lung cancer kills more men than women because of past differences in smoking habits. It is worrying to note that lung cancer is increasing in women as smoking patterns change and, in some areas, has overtaken breast cancer as the most common cause of cancer death. This is tragic for a condition which is so easily preventable.

BREAST CANCER

Breast cancer still kills more women than any other form of cancer although lung cancer is increasingly common. The causes of the disease are not fully understood although it is clearly more common in affluent societies which consume a diet rich in saturated fatty acids and where obesity is more common. A wide range of factors that increase risk has been identified. Many of these cannot be altered. The causes of the condition are thus multifactorial, making it very difficult to design a primary preventive programme. The main method of reducing deaths is, therefore, early detection and treatment. Screening is by mammography, an X-ray examination of the breast carried out three yearly on women over 50 in whom it is effective in detecting cancers. In women under this age the tissue of the breast is denser and screening does not produce any benefits. Whilst this may seem irrelevant to the education sector it is clear that attitudes to health are set early in life and that schools can play a major role in encouraging people to make appropriate use of health services including preventive services. In addition it is clear that many women fail to attend for screening because of fear about cancer and the implications of finding a lump. The myth of cancer as a death sentence is common, compounded by an apparent societal taboo about discussing the issue. Schools can encourage a more balanced approach to discussions about cancer, its prognosis and to death.

CERVICAL CANCER

Cervical cancer kills about 1,500 women a year. A high proportion could be prevented if the UK cervical screening service were as effective as the best in the world. Unlike breast cancer, where the screening programme aims to detect and treat early established cancer, the cervical screening programme aims to detect changes which precede the development of cancer and thus permits intervention before cancer can develop. Deaths now occur mainly in women who have never had a smear and who present for treatment when cancer is already established. In addition to the concerns about screening programmes discussed above, some women have been discouraged from using the service because of publicity about the sexual nature of the disease. It is clear that women who have never been sexually active do not develop the disease and that women who have had a number of sexual partners are at most risk. This has unfortunately been interpreted by the more reprehensible elements of the press to mean that cervical cancer is a disease of promiscuity. This is not the case. Many women with symptoms feel afraid to seek help or tell their family or friends because they believe they will be labelled as promiscuous despite the fact that they have had only one sexual partner. This will only be addressed by better education about sex and sexuality both within the home and within a comprehensive school programme. Whilst regular cervical smears are the first line of defence the increased use of condoms will also help as there is increasing evidence that the condition is caused by a virus transmitted during intercourse.

SKIN CANCER

Skin cancer is not a common cause of death, however, the most aggressive form, melanoma, is becoming more common. Overall skin cancers kill about 1,500 people and about 28,000 people develop them each year. Exposure to ultra-violet radiation is the single most important cause and severe sunburn at an early age is particularly significant. People with a large number of moles are also at particular risk. Intervention to halt the increase must focus on encouraging sensible exposure to sunlight including the avoidance of sunburn by the use of sunscreens, progressive exposure to sunlight and the use of sun hats. These interventions are most important in children and schools could play a significant role in encouraging a sensible approach to sunlight. Regular self examination of moles to detect any changes in appearance or bleeding is also valuable.

(3) Mental illness

MENTAL ILLNESS TARGETS

17. *To improve significantly the health and social functioning of mentally ill people.*
18. *To reduce the overall suicide rate by at least 15% by the year 2000.*
19. *To reduce the suicide rate of severely mentally ill people by at least 33% by 2000.*

Mental illness is a significant cause of illness and disability. It causes about one in seven of all working days lost, uses one seventh of total NHS resources and nearly a quarter of NHS expenditure on medicines. About 40% of the population will have some sort of problem during their lifetime. Mental illness encompasses a wide range of conditions ranging in severity from mild to severe; most are curable but some lead to life long problems and disability. One manifestation of the problem can be suicide which seems to be increasing in younger men, perhaps related to increased levels of unemployment. The mental health of children and adolescents is particularly important as disorders at this stage can adversely affect the abilities and health of adults. Young people are clearly subject to considerable physical, intellectual, social and emotional pressures but have poor coping mechanisms. Boys in particular find it difficult to deal with emotional and relationship problems. Many adolescents perceive themselves to be under stress. Schools must have a key role in helping young people identify the symptoms of stress and develop appropriate coping mechanisms. The encouragement of a more open attitude to mental illness including making discussions about the issue more acceptable would be a major contribution to an issue society still finds difficult. This would reduce stigma. Schools could also consider the role and appropriateness of counselling services.

(4) Sexual health including HIV

SEXUAL HEALTH TARGETS

20. *To reduce the incidence of gonorrhoea among men and women aged 15–64 by at least 20% by 1995.*
21. *To reduce the rate of conceptions amongst the under 16s by at least 50% by the year 2000.*
22. *To reduce the percentage of injecting drug misusers who report sharing equipment in the previous 4 weeks by at least 50% by 1997 and by a further 50% by the year 2000.*

Attention has been focussed on this issue because of the occurrence of Acquired Immune Deficiency Syndrome (AIDS) caused by the Human Immunodeficiency Virus (HIV). Sexual activity can also lead to other infections and to unwanted pregnancies. A rewarding and fulfilling personal and sexual relationship does, however, make a significant positive contribution to health: the aim is to help the population achieve the latter without the risks of the former. A comprehensive approach to sexuality is required, both promoting a mature approach and teaching how risks can be minimised. Many people still find this difficult and approaches to sexuality in the UK are still less open and confident than in some other countries. There are continuing concerns about whether openly discussing sex, contraception and disease prevention will encourage young people to become more sexually active. In reality international experience suggests that openness helps young people make appropriate decisions.

HIV continues to increase in the UK. Whilst most deaths still occur in gay men newly diagnosed cases are increasingly common in heterosexual men and women; the discrepancy appears to be due to the time lag between diagnosis and death and reflects the historical pattern of the disease; ie the fact that 10 years ago HIV was predominantly a gay disease. Critics who use the pattern of death to conclude that the disease poses no risk to heterosexuals are, at best sadly misguided, and at worst, positively dangerous, as they encourage complacency amongst young people. Control of HIV will also reduce other sexually transmitted diseases and unwanted pregnancies. Strategies concentrate on the use of barrier methods of contraception and the encouragement of 'safer sex', ie non-penetrative sexual practices. It is important that these are discussed and supported in schools. Schools also make an important contribution to the development of citizenship; sexual issues are best covered as part of a comprehensive programme of personal and social responsibility. Teaching HIV prevention solely as part of a biological approach to reproduction misses the importance and value of sexual relationships to society.

A particular issue for the reduction of HIV infection is the prevention of spread amongst people who inject drugs. This group have a high level of infection and the virus is transmitted from person to person by the sharing of injecting equipment. Preventive strategies must have two components: primary prevention, encouraging young people to resist the use of drugs by resisting peer pressure and secondly, for those who choose to inject and cannot be persuaded to stop, the reduction of harm by eliminating the sharing of equipment. Both these strategies are particularly important in schools.

(5) Accidents

ACCIDENT TARGETS

23. *To reduce the death rate for accidents among children aged under 15 by at least 33% by 2005.*
24. *To reduce the death rate for accidents among young people aged 15–24 by at least 25% by 2005.*
25. *To reduce the death rate for accidents among people aged 65 or over by at least 33% by 2005.*

Accidents are the major cause of death in people under the age of 30 and also cause considerable ill-heath and disability. Although people are fatalistic about accidents it is clear that very few are due to chance and that many could be avoided. For example, the use of alcohol is a major factor in road traffic deaths of pedestrians, cyclists and car users. Prevention strategies must include environmental changes both to the home and to public places. The provision of adequate off street play areas and traffic calming measures could be important as could the provision of simple safety equipment, for example, stair gates, in the home. Reduction of deaths and ill-health will require a multiagency approach. Schools can assist both by ensuring their own environment and procedures are adequate and by helping children identify and deal with potential hazards.

Local health strategies

By choosing to focus on diseases, the *Health of the Nation* paradoxically, requires the integration of all three approaches to prevention (namely, the medical model, the life-style model and the societal model). The goal of reducing deaths, reducing the numbers of people developing disease or ameliorating the effects of established disease, will require a wide range of interventions including both societal changes and 'high-tech' medical interventions. A range of new alliances and partnerships is necessary; no single agency or group can make an impact alone. One interesting development that is evident in many places is the emergence of working parties on health issues that, in addition to representatives from other statutory agencies, also include the people who will consume the services offered. This is very new to the medical profession and is an experience that is not altogether comfortable for, or welcomed by, many doctors. It is clear, however, that many preconceptions are already being challenged. This must be welcomed.

Health authorities are developing local health strategies based on alliances with other agencies. Schools, teachers and education authorities should be key contributors to this process and should take a broad, holistic view of the well-being of the children they serve. Health authorities have a responsibility to facilitate the process and have expertise in many of the important areas. They can ensure that strategies are firmly grounded on evidence of benefit. Most have access to staff and material resources which can be used to support other sectors. In particular they are well placed to provide training on health issues for key groups. A special contribution could potentially be made by school nurses (see Chapter 8). Most schools continue to have a trained nurse identified. The traditional role of the nurse was limited to simple health surveillance. In many authorities the role is now being extended to encompass health promotion and disease prevention. This expert resource is thus readily accessible to schools and teachers. Similarly local general practitioners are actively involved in health promotion activities targeted at the adult family members of school children. It would not be difficult to develop close links which would be beneficial to both parties.

It is important to stress that teachers, in particular, can add considerably to the process. They have access to the most vulnerable but most important sector of society; they have expertise in the best ways of imparting information and ideas to children; they contribute to the social and psychological development of young people and not merely to intellectual enhancement; they have access to parents as well as children. Any strategy that neglects this potential contribution will be sub-optimal. Teachers should be encouraged to accept these broader responsibilities, most of which require an attitude of mind rather than extra resources. A strategy which harnesses this potential energy has a real chance of success in improving the health of the next generation.

References

Aldridge, J. (1993) *Children Who Care* Loughborough University.
Alma Ata USSR (1978) *Report of the International Conference on Primary Health Care* Geneva: WHO.
Black, D. (1980) *Equalities and Inequalities in Health* London: DHSS.
Department of Health (1992) *Effect of Tobacco Advertising on Tobacco Consumption (The Smee Report)* London: HMSO.
Department of Health (1992) *Health of the Nation* London: HMSO.

38

Department of Health and Social Security (DHSS) (1987) *Promoting Better Health* London: HMSO.

Donaldson, R. and Donaldson, L. (1983) *Essential Community Medicine* Lancaster: MTP.

Health Department of Great Britain and Northern Ireland (1976) *Prevention and Health: Everybody's Business* London: HMSO.

Health Education Authority (1993) *Response to the Smee Report* London: HEA

Judge, K. and Benzeval, M. (1993) 'Health inequalities: new concerns about the children of single mothers', *British Medical Journal*, 306, pp.677–680.

Miller, B. (1993) 'Money to burn', *Health Services Journal*, 12 August.

National Opinion Poll (NOP) Market Research (1987, 1988, 1989) *Office for Population Census Surveys* London: OPCS.

O'Neill, P. (1983) *Health Crisis 2000* Oxford: Heinemann Medical Books.

Townsend, J. (1992) 'Price and taxation as preventive medicine', *HFA 2000 News*, Faculty of Public Health Medicine, Autumn 1992, No 20.

Welsh Health Planning Forum (1989) *Strategic Intent and Direction for the NHS in Wales* Cardiff: Welsh Office Publicity Unit.

Whitehead, M. (1992) 'The health divide', in Townsend, P. and Davidson, N. (eds) (1992) *Inequalities in Health* London: Penguin.

WHO (1985) *Targets for Health For All* Copenhagen: WHO Regional Office for Europe.

CHAPTER 4

The Process and Practice of Health Education

Counselling Skills in the Classroom

Sylvia McNamara

The teaching and learning skills that are useful in the teaching of health education are many and varied. However, it is clear from literature on health education that certain types of teaching are likely to be more useful than others. *Curriculum Guidance 5* highlights the importance of education to assist decision-making and raising self-esteem. Teachers are well aware that while didactic methods may be suitable for factual information and knowledge acquisition, for concept formation and deeper understanding, student-centred methods are more suitable. It is this deeper understanding that is needed for decision-making which accounts for the emphasis on student-centred and active learning methods in health education materials.

Sanctions and moralising lectures can establish an external locus of control, whereby students refrain from experimentation for fear of external repercussions. In order to develop the high order decision-making skills required to resist offers of cigarettes or to have sensible and safe approaches to alcohol use or sex experimentation, it is necessary to establish an internal locus of control where the students' behaviours are driven by internalised values.

The theoretical framework underpinning the kinds of exercises, activities and strategies offered in health education manuals is often not made explicit to teachers. This means that teachers are unable to be as successful as they might be in passing on to the students the reasons for doing the exercises, both in terms of deep understanding of health-related issues and in terms of skills acquisition for now and for later life. There are, for example, numerous activities in the manuals on 'how to listen well' (Hopson and Scally, 1981; Button, 1981; Ewles and Simnett, 1991; Clarity Collective, 1991) though the purpose of these may not always be clear to the students.

Both the research evidence and responses from young people themselves indicate that not only are lessons that revolve around information, worksheets and lectures on morality ineffective but so too are endless experiential exercises where the point, purpose and relationship to the skills needed to deal with real drug and sex experimentation situations are not explained. In this chapter I shall examine the theoretical framework of counselling skills and reflect on their contribution to teaching and learning skills for health education.

Counselling skills

These are the behaviours and communication skills which can help people to understand themselves and to become more effective as individuals. This process of helping through speaking will usually result in either insight or behavioural change or both. A definition of counselling put forward by the British Association for Counselling is: 'to give the client an opportunity to explore, discover and clarify ways of living more resourcefully and towards greater well-being' (BAC, 1984). One of the important tenets of the counselling approach is that clients start to take responsibility for themselves. This issue of personal responsibility has to be an aim of health educators for their students, because most of the health-related activities take place out of the classroom and outside of the supervision of adults. It is important to make a distinction between the type of listening and talking that goes on in: a conversation; an advice-giving session; an information or instruction session; a counselling situation.

Some teachers when reading this chapter may be thinking 'but I do not need to learn how to listen, my children can talk to me and I listen to them'. Counselling involves a special sort of listening – 'active listening'. The counsellor acts as a mirror while the client tries to identify the heart of the problem and what might be done about it. While counselling may be useful in coping with trauma, it also has wider applications. I often seek out my friends who have these skills when I want to explore several options in order to make a decision, or when I want to set myself targets, and it is precisely this skill that we want young people to acquire for healthy lives. In fact it is this target setting skill that GPs despair of ever inculcating in the public when the government exhorts doctors to reduce the incidence of smoking.

Carl Rogers (1951, 1967, 1980) was the person who developed most fully the idea of person-centred work and counselling. His ideas have been developed into a skills-based approach by Egan (1982). The skills of counselling have been made more accessible for teachers by Langham and Parker (1988) and Mallon (1991). A good summary of these ideas is presented by Nelson-Jones (1984, 1986). Rogers' work centres on what he calls his 'core conditions' and there is a significance for the educator in considering these three conditions:

RESPECT OR 'UNCONDITIONAL POSITIVE REGARD'

Rogers thought it critical for the counsellor to respect and accept the client even if the client's values or behaviours are at odds with those of the counsellor. The important thing is to suspend judgement. The results of a recent survey (Balding, 1992) show that students interviewed were ignorant of fundamental factual information about sex-related matters which produced other conceptual misunderstandings. It is not necessarily the case that these students had not been 'taught sex education'.

What often happens when we are in a group is that we operate selective listening. We can tune out information that we find embarrassing, or that we think we know already or, more likely, that we think our peers think we ought to know. Thus the suspension of judgement by both the teacher and the peer group in the classroom is crucial if students are to venture to discuss their real feelings, and if they are to state opinions or make statements. In classrooms where the climate is being carefully attended to and the class teacher has taught listening skills based on counselling psychology, and has framed rules for the classroom that encourage constructive feedback, students may then disclose their real feelings and express views which they know may get challenged by their peers, or corrected by others, if factually incorrect.

GENUINENESS OR OPENNESS

According to Rogers counsellors need to declare their own feelings, reactions to and observations of the client. Can we assume that these aims are realistic in the classroom? There is currently a debate about where health education should appear in the curriculum and who should teach it. My own position on this is unequivocal. Ideally sensitive issues such as sex education and drug education need to be taught by every member of staff, not just specialists, otherwise children grow up with the idea that the subjects are taboo, and that they can only talk to 'experts' who may not be there when they want to talk to someone.

However, I do recognise that in the present climate it would not be possible to train all staff in the methodology outlined in this chapter and elsewhere in the book, although in primary schools the question of expertise is vexed. Many primary schools are not big enough to afford the luxury of one specialist. One solution may be to leave the teaching of sensitive matters to years 5 and 6. However, the research evidence shows that this may be leaving the teaching of alcohol- and smoking-related behaviour too late. The health-related behaviour questionnaire, 1991–92, showed that 23.6% of year 4 boys and 17.5% of year 4 girls had had an alcoholic drink since the same time the previous week (Balding and Shelley, 1993).

Another alternative open to primary schools is to segregate children specifically for some sensitive issues. The problem here is that such grouping conveys an air of importance, or difference, or possible censure, concerning such health-related matters. This is the very opposite of the kinds of attitudes we want to encourage in young people if they are to take on the behaviour associated with responsible decision-making.

The call for experts to deal with health-related sensitive issues seems to be linked to the fear many teachers have of being asked tricky or personal questions. Such fears can be allayed by encouraging students to voice their own fears rather than projecting them on to the teacher. This can be done by both the teacher modelling openness and genuineness in the classroom and the teacher encouraging the students to be open and genuine with each other. Thus a climate of trust and respect is established. It is then unlikely that students will try to catch the teacher out by deliberately asking embarrassing questions. Indeed many teachers I have worked with have reported examples of peer censure and protection of the teacher when they have used this style of teaching.

EMPATHY

Again Rogers saw it as crucial for the counsellor to come to see the world in the way the client does. Whilst difficult to achieve, this is undoubtedly a skill many teachers would like their students to learn, exhibit and develop. Empathy between generations and between different sexes, racial, religious, and cultural groups leads to respect and tolerance. In classrooms where respect and tolerance exist young people are more likely to develop high self-esteem. Those with high self-esteem are shown to experience fewer problems with health-related behaviours (see Rice, 1990).

It would be possible for educators to take these three core conditions and work out ways in which they deliver the curriculum so that the core conditions are at work in their classrooms. This has clear training implications, but when teachers I have worked with have done this they have been pleasantly surprised at the increase of 'on-task' behaviour that emerges as the students begin to relate to one another in a positive and supportive way. In addition to the on-task benefits in such classrooms anxieties or confessions about health-related issues are more likely to be expressed and so too is an interest in resolving them.

The assumption in Egan's approach to counselling is that there are stages that people need to go through in order to be ready to engage in problem-solving. An awareness of the stages might be useful for the educator in several respects; one is that the students themselves will need to work through these stages in order to help one another, the other is that the class as a whole will need to be taken through these stages, in order both to establish a supportive climate and to learn the skills for each stage. The stages in the counselling relationship are expanded below.

Stating the problem

It may be that encouraging young people to state the problem is a long term goal for many teachers of health education, for example, to get students who are addicted to nicotine to see this addiction as a problem that they want to deal with. In the short term, published teaching materials, eg simulated problems or situations such as 'problems with parents', might be used so that students can practise both explaining a problem and using the skills needed to help someone else explain a problem. In the explanation, as the need to be specific and detailed becomes clear so, too, will the need for particular vocabulary in relation to health-related matters. The clarification that ensues will ensure that factual or conceptual misconceptions are dealt with as part of the listening process.

Many of the teachers and student teachers who come to courses on counselling and communication skills, assume that they need these skills themselves in order to counsel their students. They feel frustrated about the lack of time to explore problems even when they have acquired the skills. One solution to this is to teach the skills to the young people themselves, whatever their age.

Exploring the problem

The skills that need to be taught include posture, showing interest and trust and being positive. In good posture a 'knee-to-knee' rule is useful with primary school children, while 'back-to-back' listening exercises soon establish the need for facing each other and giving appropriate eye contact. The skills of summarising, paraphrasing and asking open questions need to be introduced one by one in carefully graded ways, with plenty of opportunity for practice. The reason for the students learning these skills is because the skills are those needed to show the speaker that you are interested in them, and for convincing them that they can trust you and that what you say is true. In these kinds of listening pairs it will be more likely that students will voice their feelings and perhaps some of the dilemmas they face that would otherwise often only get addressed through episodes of television programmes, such as *Brookside* or *EastEnders*. The real conflict between 'what I know I ought to do' (moral position) and 'what I actually think I will do', is the heart of many problems in the health education curriculum.

The skills of constructive feedback (saying positive things to one another – about appearance, friendships, helping behaviour, social successes) are effective for raising self-esteem. Peer pressure is a very real and difficult issue for all children to deal with, but particularly for adolescents. Even those who are high achievers in sport and consequently have respect from their peers socially, have reported the enormous difficulty of ordering non-alcoholic drinks in the pub the day of a match or the night of training. If it is so hard for young people who experience great success in an important, socially recognised, area of their lives, how much more difficult for those who believe they have no successes in any areas of their lives to resist peer pressure? This perceived lack of success in life is known as low self-esteem. It can be tackled by controlling the feedback given to children with low self-esteem from their peers, and by encouraging disclosures and positive statements as outlined above.

There are many ideas for teaching primary age children the skills of listening and responding in *Skills for the Primary School Child* (TACADE, 1990, 1993). Further ideas for work with secondary students can be found in Ryder and Campbell (1988) and Hamblin (1986) in addition to those given earlier in this chapter. It is possible to combine the teaching of these skills with the delivery of the National Curriculum, because they are the skills needed for effective groupwork (McNamara and Moreton, 1993).

Problem-solving and action planning

Peer tutoring can be a highly effective way of getting the kinds of behavioural change that health educators in both the medical and educational world aim for but often despair of achieving, for example, helping students to stop smoking, drink less, and abstain from hard drugs when offered them in social situations. Teachers have reported successes in behavioural change when students are explicitly taught skills of peer tutoring and target setting which are derived from counselling processes. However, such behavioural changes can only occur with a deep understanding of health-related issues and when students can identify for themselves that these are their own goals and their own problems.

For example, if students identify lack of exercise as a problem, they may initially set an unrealistically high goal of running three miles every day, then fail and feel even worse about it. In talking to a peer and having the help of teachers to learn to set small realistic targets, with built in support and rewards, they may arrange with a friend that they will both use the same exercise video tape in their separate homes in the morning before school, three times a week, and telephone each other immediately they have completed, or support each other with reminders of the next day if they do not manage it. Successful completion of three times in a week leads to a reward as planned by the pair in advance.

Indeed an article by Rose (1990) highlighted an interesting way of using peer pressure in a positive way. The 'stub club' was formed by a group of year 10 pupils with the aim of 'helping other younger children understand the harm that smoking does'. The club successfully presented two sessions on this theme in a local primary school.

Conclusion

Many teachers may think that they need training to improve their own knowledge levels of health-related matters. Whilst knowledge is important, and it is possible to improve one's knowledge by reading, the training need is actually largely in methodology. There is a clear need for teachers to be trained to use the counselling approach. The idea that all teachers should be health education teachers and have training in this methodology may at first seem an unrealistically expensive goal. When it is recognised that the approach has applications beyond health education, the training may not seem so expensive. What is being recommended in this chapter is a widening of the repertoire of teaching methods, that every teacher can confidently call upon in the classroom, to include the teaching of counselling skills to young people. This will mean a greater likelihood of the deep understanding which leads to both behavioural change and an internalisation of concepts and values taking place in all curriculum subjects.

References

BAC (British Association of Counselling) (1984) *Definition of Terms*, BAC, 1 Regent Place, Rugby, Warwickshire CV2 1PJ.

Balding, J. (1992) *Young People in 1992* Exeter University.

Balding, J. and Shelley, C. (1993) 'A health-related peep at 7,852 very young people', *Education and Health*, **11** (3), 43–47.

Button, L. (1981) *Group Tutoring for the Form Tutor* London: Hodder and Stoughton.

Clarity Collective (1991) *Taught Not Caught* Wisbech: Learning Development Aids.

Egan, G. (1982) *The Skilled Helper* Monterey, California: Brookes Cole.

Ewles, L. and Simnett, I. (1991) *Promoting Health: Practical Guide to Health Education* Oxford: John Wiley.

Hamblin, D. (1986) *A Pastoral Programme* Oxford: Basil Blackwell.

Hopson, B. and Scally, M. (1981) *Lifeskills Teaching Programmes Nos 1, 2, 3, 4* Leeds: Lifeskills Associates.

Langham, M. and Parker, V. (1988) *Counselling Skills For Teachers* Framework Press.

Mallon, B. (1991) *An Introduction to Counselling Skills for Special Education* Manchester: Manchester University Press.

McNamara, S. and Moreton, G. (1993) *Teaching Special Needs: Strategies and Activities for Children in the Primary Classroom* London: David Fulton Publishers.

Nelson-Jones, R. (1984) *Personal Responsibility Counselling and Therapy: an Integrative Approach* London: Cassell.

Nelson-Jones, R. (1986) *Human Relationship Skills, Training and Self-help* London: Cassell.

Rice, B. (1990) 'Promoting self-esteem in schools' in *The Manual of Skills for the Primary School Child* Salford: TACADE.

Rogers, C. (1951) *Client Centred Therapy: its current practice, implications and theory* London: Constable.

Rogers, C. (1967) *On Becoming a Person: a therapist's view of psychotherapy* London: Constable.

Rogers, C. (1980) *A Way of Being* Boston, Mass: Houghton and Mifflin.

Rose, M. (1990) 'Pupils learn to be smoking educators', *Education and Health*, **8**, 65–69.

Ryder, J. and Campbell, L. (1988) *Balancing Acts in Personal, Social and Health Education* London: Routledge and Kegan Paul.

TACADE (1990) *Skills for the Primary School Child* Salford: TACADE.

TACADE (1993) *Skills for the Primary School Child Part 2 Supplementary Cards* Salford: TACADE.

Active Learning Strategies

Neil Kitson

As the debate relating to health education and its role within the contemporary curriculum develops it is inevitable that the potential modes of delivery are assessed. Earlier this century, a review of education in Northamptonshire schools (1935) placed great store by the fact that not only were the children being taught about matters of hygiene but that they were also capable of demonstrating this through recall when asked to do so. It is clear from accounts of the time that the modes of teaching were far from active and that the main purpose of the teaching was that of imparting factual information linked to a general morality governing behaviour. Today we see health education as more than the transmission of facts. *Curriculum Matters 6* on health education sees that in today's educational system the

'... tasks for schools are to support and promote attitudes, practices and understanding conducive to good health' (HMSO, 1986).

The view of health education being more than just giving the information is built upon and developed in *Curriculum Guidance 5*.

'The emphasis in most health education curricula is on encouraging individual responsibility, awareness and informed decision-making. It is widely recognised that the provision and acquisition of information alone is unlikely to promote healthy, or discourage unhealthy behaviour' (NCC, 1990c, p.7).

It is clear from this that it is important to help young adults make informed choices about their lives rather than just encouraging them to learn the facts. One of the most effective ways of doing this is through active learning. Shor (1992) supports the benefits of this active approach when he cites Piaget who insisted on the relation of action to knowing:

'Knowledge is derived from action ... To know an object is to act upon it and to transform it ... To know is, therefore, to assimilate reality into structures of transformation and these are the structures that intelligence constructs as a direct extension of our actions' (Piaget cited in Shor, 1992, p.17).

We learn by doing and by thinking about our experiences. It is here that active learning methods make a significant contribution. In *Action Aids* Ackroyd (1990) presents a compelling rationale for the use of active learning techniques in HIV education by pointing to the lack of significant changes in behaviour as a result of the government's advertising campaign in the mid-eighties *Don't die of ignorance*. Ackroyd used a range of active learning strategies in order to get children to confront their decisions relating to HIV infection. They felt that it was not their function to preach but rather to inform through interactive structures such as role play. The advantages of such active involvement were also recognised in *Curriculum Guidance 5*:

> '... that for a health education programme to be effective it should display ... lessons which encourage the active involvement of pupils and which allow them to take some responsibility for organising their own learning' (NCC, 1990c, p.29).

There is a great range of strategies that are loosely collected under the title of active learning. All are powerful and effective teaching methods that are extremely valuable in the context of health education.

> '... much of the teaching in health education will be based on the direct involvement of pupils. Teaching methods particularly suited to this kind of approach include games, simulations, case studies, role plays' (NCC, 1990c, p.7).

What follows is a categorisation from Jones (1988) of some active learning styles.

DISCUSSIONS

These are activities in their own right and are not integral to other forms such as games. They are usually structured in some way and range from informal discourse to formal debate. They are, however, more than simple 'chats'.

EXERCISES

The participants have roles of learners, students, researchers, puzzlers and problem-solvers. Exercises can include case studies, problems which are either closed or open-ended, brief tasks or long term projects. These strategies are introduced to develop objectivity and impartiality.

GAMES

To be a game the people involved must all recognise the activity as a game and must think and behave as players trying to win whilst conforming to a set of defined rules.

SIMULATION

These are events in which the participants have functional roles and have sufficient information and enough key facts to enable them to behave with professional intent. They frequently have a predetermined goal or outcome and when repeated will follow a similar path.

ROLE PLAYS AND DRAMA

Unlike simulations these are open ended, episodic and operate in the 'as–if'. Participants are not acting or mimicking, rather they are thinking as if they were the individuals being represented. The work can use the immediate group of participants as audience – self as audience (Boulton, 1988) – or it can be presented to other members of the larger group. There is no defined outcome. All role play is drama but not all drama is role play. There is a wide range of techniques or conventions available (Neelands, 1992) to enhance, deepen and extend the students' work.

Active learning techniques in the context of health education offer ways of learning which are not there simply to cover the wide range of components in *Curriculum Guidance 5*. They offer empowerment to the participants. Shor (1992) stresses the importance of such processes as not only do they provide the most effective and permanent form of learning but also because through such processes the students can be empowered to control their own learning. With respect to health education, when using active learning one is not assuming previous knowledge on the part of the pupils, for example, concerning substance use and misuse; rather, one is setting up an activity which allows them to think and consider the range of potential effects and outcomes. Such empowerment enables individuals to recognise the existing knowledge, skills and understanding that they bring with them to the lesson and to use it, test it out and build upon it within the context of the activities that have been set up.

To illustrate this, during the development of some work on HIV education, teachers of a group of 13 year old girls suggested that looking in depth at the issue of condoms would be inappropriate as the girls would not have sufficient understanding of the subject. A simple game of 'True/False/Don't Know' based on information relating to HIV resulted in five pupils standing in the middle of the group debating the merits of safety standards 'kite' marks as they related to condoms. This was an aspect of their learning which, if left to the teachers, by their own admission, may well have been left untouched. In the event the active learning process had helped the pupils to define their own learning needs whilst at the same time recognising and giving value to what they already knew. Thus it can be seen that active learning has the potential to enable teachers to adjust the emphasis of what is taught to the extent that

'... curriculum content will be tailored by schools to match the maturity and needs of their pupils' (NCC, 1990c, p.11).

The use of active learning strategies offers participants distance and

safety. Through engaging in such activities we are looking at the relationship between the objective and subjective conditions of the experience
(Kolb, 1984). We are not concerned with the reality of events, rather the
activity becomes the metaphor for those real events (Boulton, 1986) and it
is this activity we look at and reflect upon. It offers the freedom to test out
ideas, 'create' other people or explore other view points yet maintaining
one's own notion of self (Ackroyd, 1991) without directly confronting or
directly challenging those things that are significant to us. When the activity is over, be it a game or a role play, nothing has changed, nothing has
altered. It is through reflecting upon what occurred during the activity that
learning takes place. In the simulation I can be the person in the shop who
has no regard for health care being challenged by an irate customer; in the
role play I can be the angry parent not wanting my child to be out late.
Through the active participation I am not just being informed as to what to
do, I can feel what it is like to step into someone else's shoes and to see the
world as they see it and at the end of the activity have a greater understanding as to the issue and why people react as they do.

> 'To learn is not the special preserve of a single realm of human func-
> tioning such as cognition or perception. It involves the integrated
> functioning of the total organism – thinking, feeling, perceiving and
> behaving' (Kolb, 1984, p.31).

The development of active learning techniques as part of health education does more than simply enliven the students' experience and develop an
empathetic response (Kolb, 1984). It can challenge existing assumptions,
question outcomes and enable students to confront the consequences of
their decisions (Ackroyd, 1991). The role play at key stage 4, that results in
parents turning out of home the young teenager who might be HIV positive, can be extended so that the students have to face up to the
consequences of this decision. When children in a drama at key stage 1,
in role as people looking after the doctor's surgery, decide to lock up all
the dangerous medicines for safety, not giving any to anyone until the
doctor comes back, then meet the sick old woman who desperately needs
medicine, they must face the consequences of their actions.

The health education curriculum needs to encourage individual responsibility, awareness and informed decision-making, and, as has been stated
earlier, the provision of information alone is unlikely to promote healthy or
discourage unhealthy behaviour.

If health education is to help individuals make informed choices, to
establish a health conscious life-style and to build a system of values, then
teaching methods are as important as the content of the lessons (NCC,
1990c). To meet such requirements it is essential that much of the teaching
in health education be based on the active involvement of the children.

References

Ackroyd, J., Bason, D., Cubit, B., Kitson, N., Smith, J. and Tucker, S. (1991) *Action Aids: An Interactive Learning Resource* London: Hodder and Stoughton.

Boulton, G. (1986) *Selected Writings in Drama in Education* London: Longman.

DES (1986) *Curriculum Matters 6: Health Education from 5–16* London: HMSO.

Jones, K. (1988) *Interactive Learning Events* London: Kogan Page.

Kolb, D. (1984) *Experiential Learning* Englewood Cliffs: Prentice Hall.

Neelands, J. (1990) *Structuring Drama Work* Cambridge: C.U.P.

Northamptonshire LEA (1935) *Survey of Teaching in Northamptonshire* Northants LEA.

Scott, D. and Ruddock, R. (1989) *Education and Experience* Centre for Adult and Higher Education, University of Manchester.

Shor, I. (1992) *Empowering Education* London: The University of Chicago Press.

The Role of Recording Achievement

David Tomley

Relationships are central both to health education and the recording of achievement. Much learning that takes place during the compulsory years of schooling is mediated by teachers, but the learning is done by the learners themselves. The processes of negotiated reviewing and planning that are central to recording achievement give a degree of control and responsibility for the learning to the learner and, therefore, can be a significant motivator, giving feelings of worth and of being valued and, therefore, of esteem and confidence.

One of the hoped for outcomes of a coherent programme of health education is that the learners develop such confidence and have positive views of themselves and a regard for others. By promoting the use of the recording of achievement processes across the school, individuals are able to develop a healthier, more open attitude towards situations, people and views that differ from their own presently held ones.

There is general agreement about the principles underpinning recording achievement and they are well documented (DES/WO, 1987; Smith, 1989; TEED, 1991). They are congruent with the objectives of a successful health education programme and include:

- involving the student in their own learning;
- encouraging the student to take responsibility for their learning through the process of taking stock, reflecting upon and reviewing what they have done and planning the next steps – often in discussion and consultation with someone who has a wider perspective than themselves;
- integrating the assessment into the learning process;
- facilitating the continuity of learning between all phases of an individual's life.

These principles encourage active learning styles and habits that can promote life long learning. To be effective, the students need to be taught how to be assertive, to be able to marshall evidence and arguments to support a case, to be persuaded that there are alternative views to those that they presently hold – that is, to have the necessary skills to promote the mental well-being advocated as an essential feature of health education.

For the recording of achievement processes to be effective in connection with the assessment, reporting and recording of the knowledge, skills and attitudes developed through the school's health education programme, the aims, objectives and targets for each year of the programme of study have to be known and widely available to staff and students. There has to be a co-ordinated scheme of work developed with the co-operation of all staff and the knowledge and support of both governors and parents. This scheme will in its turn be delivered by all members of staff who need to feel that it has status and the full and unequivocal support of the Senior Management Team, particularly the headteacher (NCC, 1990c).

Schools will have health education programmes for each of the key stages applicable to them. It is likely that some will be met through particular subject areas, but others will cross the subject boundaries in making their contribution to the whole curriculum. However they are met it is important that the expectations are made known through generally available and accessible schemes of work, in exactly the same way as any subject department makes its schemes of work available. Arguably, it is even more vital that a theme like health education, that is likely to be delivered through a selection of subject departments and possibly pastoral tutors too, has its yearly schemes of work particularly easily accessible. The use of curriculum maps enables the expectations to be in the public domain, accessible to governors, teachers, parents and students alike. Whichever method of implementing the health education programme that the school decides upon, there have to be ways of monitoring what has been covered and evaluating the learning (DES, 1986). The processes of recording of achievement (RoA) through regular stock-taking and review, enable both a monitoring and evaluation of the school's programme and of the pupils' learning while at the same time involving the pupils in the processes of monitoring and evaluation. The RoA process enables pupils' views to be considered alongside others when the programme is being developed so that something of a negotiated curriculum is enacted. A central aim of work with young people is to encourage them to take responsibility for their own actions and life-style. Valuable opportunities occur for this in connection with health education, none more so than in the development of the school's sex education programme. The National Children's Bureau recommends that 'the needs and opinions of young people are sought and fully considered' when such programmes are being devised (Sex Education Forum, 1992, p.13 and p.27).

In most schools, the recording of achievement began in association with the pastoral curriculum, in which health education has often featured (OU/Bristol University, 1987). However there has recently been a significant movement of the process into the subject domains. The making more open through the National Curriculum of the Attainment Targets, levels and schemes of work in all subjects; the more general availability of assessment criteria associated with course modules; the broadening of assessment procedures to include elements of course work and specific assignments, has each added to the value of the recording of achievement processes and have encouraged its take-up in more and more aspects of school life. Beyond compulsory schooling too, the process is becoming normal practice in further and higher education, training and employment (TVEI/Training Agency, 1990).

In addition to the Records of Achievement movement these trends are in line with the emphasis that is currently being placed on the individual and the change in the relationships between teachers and students, trainers and trainees and employers and employees, eg the Investors in People Initiative, individual action planning, training credits, career plans and adult guidance. Further information about all these initiatives can be obtained from Training and Enterprise Councils (TECs) in England and Wales and Local Enterprise Councils (LECs) in Scotland. It is recognised that the more that individuals are involved in their own development the better they respond. An open, honest relationship between the teachers and the students is healthier for both parties. In turn this view can be mirrored in the way that staff in the schools interact with each other as well as with the students. Schools are becoming healthier communities with an ethos of regard for individuals whatever their status. There is a partnership in learning with the student at the centre.

The management structures in schools are emphasising teamwork, recognising that the Senior Management Team is not the sole progenitor of good ideas and, therefore, promoting horizontal and upward communication channels in addition to the well used downward ones. Schools are becoming less insular. Their links with the local community via their governors, and with industry and business through work experience and teacher placements, are becoming stronger and so the school's view of itself is a more positive one and there is a real partnership at work in the life of the community.

Health education cannot be left to chance. A school needs a whole school policy for health education, it also needs one for assessment, recording and reporting. Further, it needs one that enriches the experience of all those who participate in it, one that means that people are not afraid to make difficult or uncomfortable comments provided they are based on evidence and one that in the end leads to a healthier environment for teaching and learning. As well as academic and vocational development, schools promote the personal and social growth of young people. Schools offer a protected environment where young people can explore, challenge and develop attitudes and knowledge connected with issues such as stereotyping, gender and power and to develop social and interpersonal skills. The nature of the environment in which they learn and practise these, the way in which the students themselves are treated by adults and their peers, how the teaching and learning is organised and the school managed give important messages and signals to them during an impressionable period of their lives. Where schools have open styles of management, students can be helped to recognise that they have a responsibility for some of the prevailing ethos and can directly affect some of the practices. Opportunities can be provided for discussion of such matters as bullying, sexism and racism, in a way that does not individualise problems, but gives the ability to discuss social, cultural, political and other sensitive issues in a way that leads to better understanding. Teachers do have to ensure that their interactions and discussions with students cannot be interpreted as prying or surveillance. Evidence from some year 11 students seems to indicate that adolescents may sometimes feel that teachers can be insensitive and incautious in what they ask. Pupils can also be concerned about confidentiality and security of records (Tomley, 1993). These are matters for schools to address and be aware of if a process which aims to give some responsibility and control to the learner, is seen by them as a means of checking on and controlling them.

Used appropriately, the aims of the recording of achievement process and the outcomes of an effective health education programme are entirely consistent. They reinforce each other. Indeed, a great opportunity is missed if both are not implemented together to the advantage of students and staff who make up the community of the school.

References

DES (1986) *Curriculum Matters 6: Health Education from 5 to 16* London: HMSO.

DES/WO (1987) *Records of Achievement: Interim Report* London: HMSO.

Open University/Bristol University (1987) *Pilot Records of Achievement in Schools Evaluation (PRAISE) Interim Evaluation Report* Milton Keynes: Open University.

Sex Education Forum (1992) *An Enquiry into Sex Education* London: National Children's Bureau.

Smith, G (1989) 'Principles into practice', *Education*, **173** (21), 494–496.

TVEI/Training Agency (1990) *Guidance for Those Managing TVEI Recording Achievement and Planning Individual Development (RAPID)* Training Agency, Moorfoot, Sheffield.

Tomley, D. (1993) *Individual Action Plans – An Evaluation: Final Report of the Extension Phase of the Lincolnshire Youth Development Project* Lincolnshire County Council.

Training Enterprise and Education Directorate (TEED) (1991) *Quality Assurance and the National Record of Achievement* Employment Department, Moorfoot, Sheffield.

CHAPTER 5

Health Education and the Cross-curricular Themes

Economic and Industrial Understanding

Alan Sutton

According to *Curriculum Guidance 4*, Economic and Industrial Understanding (EIU) has the ambitious aim of enabling pupils to make informed economic decisions with which they will be faced throughout their life. As such the theme makes a particular contribution to preparing young people for a variety of roles in adult life and work – as producers, consumers and citizens. Prior to the official announcement of the five themes, both health education and EIU figured prominently in the curriculum although they differed in the extent to which they permeated the curriculum as a whole. Health education was one of ten controversial issues identified by Stradling (1984) in a research study in the early 1980s.

The promotion of EIU was closely related to attempts by the government and some large employers to vocationalise the school curriculum, a process which had started in the late 1970s but given a major boost by the introduction of the Technical and Vocational Educational Initiative (TVEI) in 1982. Increasingly fuelled by concerns about the lack of the UK's international competitiveness, the purpose of this vocational movement was to prepare young people for adult and working life by fostering skills which employers needed as well as changing attitudes to industry. TVEI was largely responsible for a work-related curriculum which: included work experience for all students aged 14-16; EIU courses or components as part of a PSE programme; and encouraged the industrial applications of particular subjects.

As indicated in the introduction to this book the five cross-curricular themes overlap and they are all underpinned by the cross-curricular dimensions and skills. The publication of the NCC guidance on cross-curricular themes in 1990 was intended to help schools plan, manage and teach the themes. In the case of health education, although the theme is broad, internal coherence is assisted by the identification of nine components and there are suggestions in *Curriculum Guidance 5* as to how these topics can be covered throughout the four key stages. Of the nine health education components, five have links with all the other four themes. Those which appear particularly relevant to EIU are the use and abuse of substances, health and safety, environmental health and diet and nutrition.

Economic understanding, as defined by *Curriculum Guidance 4,* is the ability to consider how an economy's scarce resources might best be used. An economically literate person has the skills, information and concepts necessary to assess the implications of the decisions which people, organisations and governments make. These decisions in turn affect economic growth, living standards, employment and services and so relate to all the other themes. *Curriculum Guidance 4* identifies six areas of knowledge: concepts; business enterprise; industry and the world of work; consumer affairs; technological developments; government, economy and society. Some of these components, notably industry and work, consumer affairs, technology, and government, economy and society, provide a context for links with health education. Despite this framework, however, in EIU there is a fundamental problem of a lack of overall internal coherence, which, at first glance, makes planning with other themes difficult. The problem is particularly acute in relation to industrial understanding where there is a range of concepts (Kerr, 1994).

These economic concepts are related to the fundamental tension between the scarcity of resources and the needs of people in society. This implies that difficult decisions have to be made about how resources are used, and considered choices have to be made between alternative uses. From this stem some key concepts which have been identified in *Curriculum Guidance 4*. These are: resources; cash; needs; exchange of goods and services; production.

The understanding of these concepts is particularly relevant when planning topics or teaching controversial issues where there are clear links between EIU and health education (see Felce and Pathan, 1993; Harrison, 1993). Examples of health issues could include some of the following: the decision of some consultants not to operate on a patient who has a long history of smoking but who has paid into the National Health Service (NHS) over a long period of time; a situation in the reformed NHS where doctors are obliged to make decisions on priorities where budgets are tight; the maximising of profits in industry at the expense of health and safety of workers; the damage done to the environment and in turn to health by the emission of noxious effluent; the unequal distribution of wealth, both on a global scale, as evidenced by the gap between the north and the south, and on a local scale, between the poor and rich, which results in poor diet, malnutrition and, in extreme cases, famine; the pharmaceutical company in a monopolistic situation which appears to make huge profits; the introduction of new technology in a company and its impact on the mental and physical health of its workers.

Many of these issues are controversial, resulting in differing opinions which are sometimes difficult to resolve, either because of the lack of objective evidence or because opinions are based on different value positions. These issues are valuable because they invite students to understand the divergence of opinions, to clarify their own values and attitudes, to justify their positions, and to understand the implications of their views and in some cases actually to change their behaviour. For some writers such as Stradling (1984), this aspect of values education is critical:

> 'In our view, the litmus test of teaching controversial issues, ought to be whether pupils are more likely to question their own and others' perceptions and points of view'.

Some of these controversial issues can be explored in current topics which are already being taught in core and foundation subjects such as humanities, geography, history or science, or they can be part of a lengthier project in which adults other than teachers are used as a resource. In one school, a year group carried out a project on the issue of smoking and involved pupils in investigating: costs to the NHS of illness relating to smoking; government revenue from taxation on tobacco sales; media pressure on consumers; advertising and legislation. Visitors to the year group included a local GP, a consultant cardiologist, a tobacconist, advertising personnel and representatives of ASH (Action on Smoking and Health).

Some components of health education, notably health and safety, can be investigated on a visit to a work place or as part of work experience. One year group investigated safety at work. After an initial visit from a Health and Safety Officer from a local company, pupils visited a range of working environments to compare the regulations and their application. They looked at protective clothing, fitness for purpose, other clothing regulations and so on. The project culminated with a display of work for the parents and employees.

Another approach (COIC, 1991) is where economic 'topics' such as unemployment and the welfare state could provide a focus for a study bringing in all the cross-curricular themes. A study of employment could include an investigation into the social costs of unemployment related to health, such as drug and alcohol abuse, stress, depression and suicide. Similarly a study of the welfare state could include an investigation into the National Health Service or private medical care, looking at, among other aspects, costs, value for money, quality of service and patient opinion.

In order to maximise the potential contribution of these themes to the whole curriculum, it might be useful to conclude with some advice on planning. To establish the links between health education and EIU teachers might take account of some of the following considerations:

● inclusion of some issues which require an understanding of those EIU concepts which impact on health education to enable students to clarify their views;

- selection of some topics or issues which are directly relevant and immediate to students' lives, eg issues to do with smoking, but also, in the words of Stenhouse (1970), 'matters of widespread and enduring significance', eg the unequal distribution of wealth and its implications for health in the Third World;
- the selection of some issues which are process based in that they help students to develop core skills such as information handling, social and life skills and to develop generalisable concepts or key ideas which they can apply in other contexts;
- recognition and acknowledgement of the complexity of many of these issues and the need for students to be provided with a variety of perspectives;
- use of the resources of the local community, investing in appropriate experts and exploring and making full use of different contexts for learning, eg work experience;
- use of a range of student-centred and resource-based approaches;
- selection of examples on a local, national and international scale.

References

COIC (Careers and Occupational Information Centre) (1991) *Implementing the Whole Curriculum: EIU, Cross-curricular Themes, Skills and Dimensions, Book 5* Manchester City Education Department.

Felce, J. and Pathan, L. (1993) *Cross-curricular Theme Pack 4: EIU* Cambridge: Pearson Publishing.

Harrison, J. (1993) *Cross-curricular Theme Pack 3: Health Education* Cambridge: Pearson Publishing.

Kerr, D. (ed) (1994) *Developing Economic and Industrial Understanding in the Curriculum* London: David Fulton.

Stenhouse, L. (1970) *The Humanities Curriculum Project: An Introduction* London: Heinemann.

Stradling, R., Noctor, M. and Baines, B. (1984) *Teaching Controversial Issues* London: Edward Arnold.

Address

Action on Smoking and Health (ASH), 5–11 Mortimer Street, London W1N 7RH (Tel: 071-637-9843).

Careers Education and Guidance

Graham Robb

Health Education and Careers Education and Guidance (CEG) 'have' at least one thing in common. Both are identified in the interim report of Sir Ron Dearing (1993), and by Rowe (1993), as distinct and different from the other cross-curricular themes. Dearing specifies that time 'saved' by the slimming of the curriculum could be used for Health Education and Careers (Dearing, 1993, p.32) while the London Institute report identifies the two as the 'least permeated' of the cross-curricular themes. Why is there this view of them as different from the other cross-curricular elements? From the point of view of national policy makers and school management teams there is probably something discrete about the nature of both. For the policy makers it is perhaps to do with the political agenda of the 'Health of the Nation' policy and the National Education and Training Targets. For the school management teams the distinctiveness perhaps comes from a long history of discrete provision of the two elements in one form or other – a written policy, a designated (and paid!) co-ordinator, and perhaps (until recently) support from LEA advisory staff. But despite this tradition in CEG there is much evidence of very patchy provision of Careers Education and Guidance in schools (Cleaton, 1987; NACGT/ICG, 1993) as measured by indicators such as curriculum time, resources, allocation of qualified staff, policy statements and evaluation systems. From discussion it appears that the same pattern of patchy provision applies to health education. The proposition that this patchiness exists as a result of a lack of understanding of the conceptual base of careers work underpins the approach taken in this chapter. The conception of CEG as it relates to health education and a broader view of the curriculum will be examined. The purpose is to get beneath the often simplistic and unhelpful conception of CEG and demonstrate a common conceptual framework, not only for CEG and health education, but for the whole curriculum.

The development of a more conceptual approach to health education, as outlined in Chapter 2, forms the basis of the link between health education and CEG work in schools. The next sections will show how the same model of progression is found in effective CEG work.

Underlying principles of CEG

For some years the commonly used conceptual framework underlying CEG was summarised in the acronym DOTS:

Decision-Making
Opportunity Awareness
Transition Skills
Self Awareness

This was the basis of much curriculum innovation and development and underpinned the HMI report *Careers Education from 5–16* (HMI, 1988).

The 1988 Education Reform Act made implicit the role of CEG by placing a statutory responsibility on schools to provide a broad and balanced curriculum which:

> 'promotes the spiritual, moral, cultural, mental and physical development of pupils at the school, and of society'

and

> 'prepares pupils for the opportunities and experiences of adult life'.

Curriculum Guidance 6 (NCC, 1990d) identified five 'strands' of careers work: self, work, role, career and transition, which could be explored through five components of Careers Education and Guidance as follows :

> careers education: a planned programme for all four key stages;
> access to information;
> experience of work;
> access to individual guidance;
> recording achievement and planning for the future.

While the statement of the components is a helpful one, some practitioners still prefer to base their curriculum thinking on DOTS rather than on the National Curriculum strands which offer a less clear conceptual frame.

But there is an even more profound issue to explore and that is the conception of the underlying purpose behind careers work. Law (1992) identifies five concept clusters relating to careers work. At a crude level careers work can be based on **matching** pupils to vacancies. There is also the concept of **enabling** students to develop self-esteem and to be more self directed in dealing with opportunities arising. A further concept is the directive work which is done to coach students for the opportunities available. Another is one of **networking** in which the student is taught to make the most of the networks available to her/him, whether through a record of achievement interview or learning through community service. Finally there is the concept of **educating**, with a focus on learned behaviour. In this Law identifies learning taking place in four stages:

> gathering and organising impressions;
> checking and understanding points of view;
> dealing with problem-solving and decision-making processes;
> accepting responsibility in a situation for oneself and others.

It would seem that a conceptual approach to CEG which is based on **educating** is one which provides the most helpful pathway for development. Any other concept would seem to confine itself to operation at key stage 4, or to be insufficiently rigorous in its way of letting young people analyse the world outside themselves. Certainly any progression from ages 5–18 is limited by any other organising concept. This can be seen by referring to the HMI dimensions of progression in Careers Education and Guidance described in *Curriculum Matters 10* (HMI, 1988):

(1) sense of identity;
(2) developing physical capacities and self confidence;
(3) managing new environments;
(4) taking responsibility for decisions;
(5) handling information;
(6) increasing knowledge and experience of the world outside school.

Exemplars of a cross-curricular approach

What practice is there which demonstrates the integration of health education and CEG within a whole school framework? Within one school the following examples illustrate the blend of whole school and subject-based activities which may contribute to a balanced integration of health education and CEG within a whole school curriculum.

- The School Council discussed the Borough 'No Smoking' Policy and the impact on the school community – including teaching staff, cleaners, catering staff, organisations wishing to hire the school, and Adult Education groups. Simultaneously, a 'Stub Club' was set up by a member of staff for pupils who wished to give up smoking, which was based on the earlier work done at Raunds School in Northamptonshire (Rose, 1990, pp.65–69).
- All pupils in the school contributed to developing a Code of Conduct affecting young people and adults as members of the school community. Using *Curriculum Guidance 5* the codes include reference to: substance use; safety; environmental aspects of health education; psychological aspects of health education. As important as the detailed content was the process by which the school community identified the issues and began to resolve them.
- A year 9 Health Day involved pupils working with community workers in a range of health and leisure careers, for example, leisure centre workers, road safety officers and personal protection trainers. Pupils were learning not only skills and knowledge about the range of health and leisure areas but also about careers and the work choices which they will make.
- Groups of year 11 pupils spent a week at the regional headquarters of British Gas, developing understanding of team-building, coping with conflict, exploring industrial personnel decision-making, personal care and safety procedures.
- Pupils in each year group were briefed in science and technology

classes on safe working practice and personal care in practical environments.

- Pupils on work experience observed and recorded issues of safety and personal presentation and care within their work experience record.

Inevitably every school has its repertoire of activities which could contribute to an integrated approach to health education and CEG. But of course the problem arises as to whether these activities are an entitlement for all pupils, or whether they are experienced by self selected groups. It is, therefore, the issue of curriculum design to which we must now turn.

Curriculum design

In the past Personal and Social Education (PSE) in the curriculum often became a carrier for all the parts which cannot be fitted into other slots – in other words, it includes everything from fireworks safety to contraception. A rational approach to curriculum design should be based around the fundamental values which pupils need to explore to prepare them for their adult and working life.

A curriculum leader may now welcome some drawing together of the various concepts and practices. How does one organise a curriculum which is based on a conceptual base which helps the young person, whatever its mode of delivery? The work by Buck and Inman (1993) suggests four criteria for curriculum planning:

(1) Objectivity and the use of evidence
Examining a range of ways of life; encouraging a critical perspective; judging the quality and quantity of evidence.

(2) Using concepts
Concepts enable the learner to put experience in categories, organise them and then analyse their knowledge and experience. Key concepts include: choices, needs, wants, divisions of labour, rights and responsibilities.

(3) Participatory and experiential teaching and learning styles
The purpose here is developing skills for independent learning including personal and interpersonal, IT, communication, decision-making.

(4) Key questions to explore fundamental issues
Buck and Inman (1993) identify nine key questions including:
'What is the nature of our rights and responsibilities in everyday life?'
'In what ways are the welfare of individuals and societies maintained?'
'On what basis do people make decisions when faced with particular choices?'
'How do people organise, manage and control their relationships?'
'What is the balance between individual freedom and the constraints necessary for co-operative living?'

64

These questions explore the core values of our society and also necessarily encourage further links across the curriculum. This review of core value questions will begin to produce a holistic curriculum design.

In terms of a syllabus one can envisage a sequence of study programmes for ages 5–16 which explore these questions in a developmental way and provide the framework for more detailed exploration of specific issues in health education and in CEG as well as the other cross-curricular themes. In this way one is freed from the tyranny of a content-driven approach and can take an approach to the work which is **educating** pupils in the true sense of the concept.

References

Buck, M. and Inman, S. (1993) 'Making values central: the role of the cross-curricular themes', *Careers Education and Guidance*, NACGT.

Cleaton, D. (1987) *Survey of Careers Work* London: NACGT and Newpoint.

Dearing, R. (1993) *The National Curriculum and its Assessment: An Interim Report* London: NCC/SEAC.

HMI (1988) *Curriculum Matters 10, Careers Education from 5–16* London: HMSO.

Law, B. (1992) *Understanding Careers Work* NACGT.

NACGT/ICG (1993) *Careers Education and Guidance in British Schools* ICG.

Rose, M. (1990) 'Pupils learn to be smoking educators', *Education and Health*, Vol. 8.

Rowe, G., Aggleton, P. and Whitty, G. (1993) *Subject and themes in the School Curriculum* (Working paper for ESRC project *Assessing Quality in Cross Curricular Context*) University of London, Institute of Education.

WHO (1984) *Health Promotion: a discussion paper on the concept and principles* Copenhagen: WHO.

Further details about **The National Association of Careers and Guidance Teachers** (NACGT) can be obtained from The Membership Secretary, Mrs G. Stanton, 46 Fairfield Road, Penarth, South Glamorgan CF6 1SL.

Citizenship Education

Ken Fogelman

'Without peace and social justice, without enough food and water, without education and decent housing, and without providing each and all with a useful role in society and an adequate income, there can be no health for the people, no real growth and no social development' (WHO, 1986, p.17).

'Education is the foundation for developing individual potential and for ensuring useful participation in society. It is also a basis for making informed choices about life-styles, and for looking after personal and family health' (WHO, op cit, p.18).

These two quotations from the World Health Organisation publication, *Targets for Health for All,* provide a succinct statement of why health and citizenship issues are so interdependent. Without good health individuals will be limited in their ability to choose to play a full role as active and participating citizens. Equally, social and political contexts and structures influence the available choices and life-styles to enable individuals and groups to develop and sustain their health and, of course, education plays a vital part in providing young people with the information, understanding and skills relevant to both areas.

A similar point was made by Rowe (1991), when writing of '... serious inequities whose effect in many cases is to exclude British citizens from the exercise of their citizenship in all its scope. This ... goes to the heart of the argument about the welfare state'. As it happens, he was writing about citizenship, but could equally have been making the case for health education. Health inequalities have been a major concern in this country and beyond for some time (eg DHSS, 1980; Fox, 1989), and were a main focus of the WHO report cited above; and, of course, issues about the role and structure of the National Health Service are a major element in any 'argument about the welfare state'.

Thus, health education is not simply a matter of imparting information about appropriate behaviour and life-styles and promoting physical fitness. It must also be placed within, and build upon understanding of, the social contexts and individual value systems which may encourage or inhibit the healthy development both of the individual and of the community. In the same way, it makes no sense for schools to approach citizenship education and health education (nor indeed the other cross-curricular themes) as if they were separate entities.

NCC Guidance

The current agenda for citizenship and health education in schools in

England is set largely by the guidance issued by the National Curriculum Council, although also influential for citizenship education has been the report of the Speaker's commission on citizenship (1990). The NCC guidance for health education is described in detail elsewhere in this volume. *Curriculum Guidance 8* defines education for citizenship as developing '... the knowledge, skills and attitudes necessary for exploring, making informed decisions about and exercising responsibilities and rights in a democratic society'. It provides a suggested framework consisting of three elements: objectives, content and activities. Objectives include: knowledge (of the nature of the community, roles and relationships in a democratic society, the nature and basis of duties, responsibilities and rights); cross-curricular skills; attitudes; and moral codes and values.

For the content, eight 'essential components' are suggested, comprising: the nature of community; roles and relationships in a pluralistic society; the duties, responsibilities and rights of being a citizen; the family; democracy in action; the citizen and the law; work, employment and leisure; public services.

Common content

It is important to emphasise that the NCC documents are, as their titles make explicit, for guidance only. They provide suggested frameworks, and it is for schools to adapt them to their own needs and implement them in their own way. Paradoxically, this can enable greater stability and consistency of approach than the ever-changing statutory requirements of the core and foundation subjects. Nevertheless, their content has been generally accepted by schools as providing useful starting-points.

It is not difficult to analyse the components of health and citizenship education as suggested by NCC, and begin to identify where there is overlap and, therefore, the potential for addressing both simultaneously. Brown and Edwards (1993) have done just this, and demonstrate how there is a considerable amount of such overlap, particularly between the citizenship components 'community' and 'family life' and health components, 'family life education' and 'psychological aspects of health education'. These and other commonalities are to be found at all key stages.

A similar point can be drawn from the national survey of secondary schools carried out for the Speaker's commission (Fogelman, 1990 and 1991a). Schools were asked to indicate topics which they taught within the curriculum relevant to citizenship education. Replies included, at key stage 3, health and safety, alcohol education, eating for health, recreation, smoking, personal safety, life-styles; and at key stage 4, health morals, mental health studies, sexual relationships and decision-making, child care, handicap in the community, and child development. These are just some of the most obvious examples of topics which can be used to address issues central to both health and citizenship. Others can be found in Harrison (1993).

Of course, as Brown and Edwards emphasise, the common ground between health and citizenship education is not only in terms of knowledge content. They write also of the importance of encouraging self-confidence and self-esteem; of empowering young people and supporting their personal and social development; of appreciating values, beliefs and moral codes and how these change over time; of personal decision-making and awareness of external influences; and of respect for different ways of living, beliefs and opinions. Similarly, the list in *Curriculum Guidance 5* of pupils' abilities to be developed within health education applies equally as well to citizenship education: assessing evidence; making decisions; negotiating; listening; making and dealing with relationships; solving problems; working independently and confidently.

Policy and planning

Identifying overlaps among the cross-curricular themes, and with conventional subjects, is important, but perhaps not the most difficult task which faces schools. An NCC working paper (1992) refers to three major challenges for schools in implementing the themes; persuading staff they are relevant and necessary; dealing with issues of overlap and progression; and ensuring co-ordination.

The first of these is perhaps the most difficult. In the present climate it would be readily understandable that teachers might feel that they have more than enough to cope with in assimilating and responding to what is required by law, and decide to leave on one side, at least for the moment, what is merely suggested. However, it does appear that teachers increasingly appreciate the need to consider the fundamental purposes of the education which they provide, and the opportunities to address these which the themes provide. The main problem is that of time, and there is every reason to be optimistic that the current review of the National Curriculum will lead to significant reductions, and space for schools to use the time released to develop their own strengths and interests (Dearing, 1993).

Consideration of overlap, progression and co-ordination leads directly to the need for a whole school policy which addresses such issues in the context of an over-arching institutional view of the curriculum, both formal and informal, in general, and of cross-curricularity in particular.

Gyte and Hill (1991) have made the case for citizenship education as the integrating element for cross-curricularity, because of its particular influence on school ethos, and with the 'health promoting school as one aspect of this'. In other words, because it can provide the most general perspective on preparation for adult life, education for citizenship can subsume and provide a rationale for the other cross-curricular themes. This is certainly one valid approach, but each school will need to arrive at its own philosophy. Furthermore, we need to recognise that many schools will have substantial traditions and experience of health education, long pre-dating the National Curriculum and NCC guidance. Although, for many, citizenship education is equally not a new idea (see, for example, Batho, 1990), schools will feel more comfortable building upon their existing strengths and experiences. Alternative cross-curricular approaches and ways of developing them can be found in Harrison and Knights (1993) and in Edwards and Pathan (1993).

Through such activities we can strive to ensure that each of our pupils receives an education which is coherent, purposeful and valuable. In the last resort, it does not matter whether the labels under which this happens include health education, citizenship education or anything else. What does matter is the young people who leave our schools, their qualities and achievements, and their ability to lead healthy, fulfilled lives. As Sowden and Walker (1991) wrote of the Dukeries complex, 'We cannot actually timetable 'caring' but we can provide opportunities which arise out of individual, group teacher or student needs ... most important features such as mutuality, co-operation with others, shared responsibility and learning how to manage common goals and purposes'.

References

Batho, G. (1990) 'The history of the teaching of civics and citizenship in English schools', *The Curriculum Journal*, **1**, 1, 91–107.

Brown, T. and Edwards, J. (1993) 'Health Education' in Edwards, J. and Fogelman, K. (1993).

Dearing, R. (1993) *The National Curriculum and its Assessment: An Interim Report* York and London: NCC and SEAC.

DHSS (1980) *Inequalities in Health: Report of a Research Working Group* London: HMSO.

Edwards, J. and Fogelman, K. (eds) (1993) *Developing Citizenship in the Curriculum* London: David Fulton Publishers.

Edwards, J. and Pathan, L. (1993) *Cross-curricular INSET and Resources* Cambridge: Pearson Publishing.

Fogelman, K. (1990) 'Citizenship in Schools: A National Survey, appendix E' in Speaker's Commission on Citizenship (1990).

Fogelman, K. (1991a) 'Citizenship in Secondary Schools: the National Picture' in Fogelman (1991b).

Fogelman, K. (ed) (1991b) *Citizenship in Schools* London: David Fulton Publishers.

Fox, J. (1989) *Health Inequalities in European Countries* Aldershot: Gower.

Harrison, J. (1993) *Cross-curricular Theme Pack 3: Health Education* Cambridge: Pearson Publishing.

Harrison, S. and Knights, G. (1993) 'Cross-curricularity' in Edwards and Fogelman (1993).

NCC (1992) *Setting the Scene: Commonality in the Cross-curricular Themes* NCC working paper, March 1992.

Gyte, G. and Hill, D. (1991) 'Citizenship in schools' in Fogelman (1991b).

Rowe, A. (1991) 'Citizenship in schools: a political perspective' in Fogelman (1991b).

Sowden, R. and Walker, L. (1991) ' The Dukeries Community College and complex: a case study' in Fogelman (1991b).

Speaker's Commission on Citizenship (1990) *Encouraging Citizenship* London: HMSO.

WHO (1986) *Targets for Health for All* Copenhagen: World Health Organisation.

Environmental Education

Steve Goodall

The changing nature of our society and its wealth of health advice challenges our ideas about what constitutes the body of knowledge which we can consult when making informed decisions about our own life-styles. Some aspects of environmental education confirm pragmatic, common sense approaches to health education whilst others highlight the problems of having access to a wealth of information, some of it conflicting. We are encouraged to achieve health and good looks by buying particular products or by adhering to particular life-styles. There has never been a more pressing need for schools to help pupils develop critical skills to aid them in decision-making.

Schools have at least two important functions to fulfil in health and environmental education. They must help pupils to question, in a reasoned and constructive way, the legitimacy of what makes up the current body of knowledge. They must help pupils acquire the skills needed to make such questions relevant and constructive.

Pupils operate in a variety of environments at school. They must be effective in intellectual, psychological, physical and social environments simultaneously. Intellectual requirements mean they need to be motivated to ask questions, process information and make decisions. Schools may already recognise the importance and relationship between psychological well-being and the physical environment in terms of aesthetics and threat to health. Socially pupils are asked to interact with their peers and the adult world considering an ever-increasing volume of information. The network of environments and citizenship communities weaves complex relationships in which pupils are asked to make decisions. They may feel under pressure to respond inconsistently and hence become confused.

Certain pragmatic features of environmental and health education still emerge which relate directly to the theme of citizenship. It is clear that individuals cannot simply please themselves. What they do affects others: hence the need for individuals to accept responsibility for their own actions. Individuals must, therefore, be able to seek out and process effectively the information available to them. The advice in *Curriculum Guidance 5* appears to fall into two categories, that of common sense and that of opportunity for discussion and development. It would seem clear that some actions by individuals are demonstrably harmful to others, eg the use of addictive substances which can affect those around them. Schools can therefore, for example, reasonably formulate No Smoking policies and offer drug education. Some other pieces of advice offering more contentious areas for debate are listed below:

At **key stage 1** it is suggested that pupils:
know that individuals are part of these environments and have some responsibility for their care; develop an understanding of how and why rules are made concerning the school and other environments.

At **key stage 2** pupils are advised:
that within any environment there are people with different attitudes, values and beliefs and that these influence people's relationships with each other and with the environment.

At **key stage 3** pupils should:
understand the impact of the media and advertising on attitudes towards health.

At **key stage 4** pupils should:
understand how legislation and political, social, economic and cultural decisions affect health;
accept responsibility for and be able to justify personal choices and decisions about health; show some insight into other people's lifestyles, values, attitudes and decisions; be aware of how food shortages and surpluses occur and the health effects of malnutrition and overconsumption;
develop a commitment to the care and improvement of their own and other people's health, community and environment.
(NCC, 1990c, pp.13–20).

In helping pupils to make decisions in the areas above, schools have the opportunity to consult a wide range of contemporary material which is challenging many of the accepted ways of thinking. The need for schools to use relevant, contemporary material when dealing with environmental issues is stressed elsewhere (Edwards and Fogelman, 1993, pp.39–42). One must consider what it is we are citizens of. The framework in which health education matters and environmental issues are approached has considerable influence upon the response of the individual. For example, those who conclude that additional transport systems damage the environment and pose hazards to health may face censure from the society they are trying to improve. Their active **citizenship** over issues such as Twyford Down poses the question of how individuals ought to act when their conclusions differ from those of processes of public enquiry and the law.

One of the most critical areas which schools face is that they are operating within a particular cultural and historical context which influences the information they may consider relevant. Only when schools consciously look outside their own fields of experience are they able to compare other cultural and historical heritages with their own (Scheffler, 1985; White and Pollak, 1986; LeVine and White, 1986). This is an essential element in schools' equality of opportunity policies but it does raise a further question as to what value system schools legitimately use as a measure of acceptable health and environmental conduct.

Other cultural views are challenging. For example, some sixty billion domesticated farm animals are killed for consumer consumption annually and every eight seconds an acre of forest is destroyed for timber or further farm land. Sixty million people world-wide will starve to death, few of them from the western, white-dominated, industrial nations (Robbins, 1990).

The industrialisation and attempted control of the land in this manner is only seen as progress if one remains within the perspective of western neo-Darwinism. From this scientific and cultural viewpoint such changes form an inevitable part of a ladder mentality in which people move from simple to complex, from instinct to rationality, from less conscious to more conscious (Lawlor, 1991, pp.18-20). We assume that change towards the more complex is progress and that with it comes heightened awareness about our environment, health and responsibilities. However, orthodox archaeological evidence suggests strongly that a hunter/gatherer style of life supported more robust individuals showing fewer signs of degenerative diseases than did the later agrarian style of life (Diamond, 1987, pp.64-66). In contrast the stress effects of some modern life-styles are aptly illustrated by Sebastian Coe's and Steve Ovett's problems with recurrent viral infections, and the deaths of eight world-class orienteers in Sweden in 1992 as described in the BBC programme, *On the Line*, 27 July 1993. The effectiveness in promoting health of aerobics, jogging and now cycling, is currently being questioned.

Schools play a crucial part in helping to form pupil attitudes. Beautiful surroundings may well be necessary for the realisation of human potential. It is part of our cultural tradition. The romantic poets reacted against the Age of Reason. Similarly conservationists and New Age thinkers perceived that technology was failing to satisfy human aspirations (Bronowski, 1973, pp.437–438). Yet there is the danger that such cultural traditions are the preserve of the fashionable, the weird or the academic. Authority cannot simply provide people with beautiful surroundings or healthy life-styles. If schools are to be a means towards a healthier society, the three components, health, environment and citizenship education have to be integrated. This enables all pupils to find ownership in common sense approaches to obvious problems. Pupils have to be helped to find ownership in, perhaps not every solution, but the process towards solutions to more contentious issues. Teachers have, therefore, to learn not to be intellectually arrogant, to listen to their pupils and when they do decide to intervene, to do so respectfully (Pantin, 1983).

The changing nature of health advice, widening access to large amounts of information and the existence of multicultural influences challenge what makes up the body of knowledge about healthy life-styles. Schools must seek to broaden their cultural and social bases in order adequately to reflect the diverse nature of the factors involved in effective education.

References

Bronowski, J. (1973) *The Ascent of Man* London: BBC.
Diamond, J. (1987) 'The Worst Mistake in the History of the Human Race', in *Discover,* May 1987.
Edwards, J. and Fogelman, K. (eds) (1993) *Developing Citizenship in the Curriculum* London: David Fulton Publishers.
Lawlor, R. (1991) *Voices of the First Day: Awakening in the Aboriginal Dreamtime* Rochester, Vermont: Inner Traditions.
Levine, R.A. and White, M.I. (1986) *Human Conditions: The Cultural Basis of Educational Developments* London: Routledge and Kegan Paul.
Pantin, G. (1983) Keynote address to *The International Community Education Association* Dublin.
Robbins, J. (1990) *Diet for a New America* Santa Cruz: Earth Save.
Scheffler, I. (1985) *Of Human Potential: An Essay in the Philosophy of Education* London: Routledge and Kegan Paul.
White, M. and Pollak, S. (1986) *The Cultural Transition: Human Experience and Social Transformation in the Third World and Japan* London: Routledge and Kegan Paul.

CHAPTER 6

Health Education and other subjects in the Curriculum

Mathematics

Rose Griffiths

Many cross-curricular themes provide opportunities for children to see that mathematics is a relevant and useful subject, but health education is a particularly rich source of contexts which interest children, and where mathematical ideas and skills are valuable.

Putting a problem into human terms can both improve motivation, and provide opportunities to test and increase children's understanding of particular mathematical ideas. For example, I watched a group of nine year-olds in one school, plodding through a worksheet of questions based on the calendar, with repetitive questions such as 'What day is five days after February 2nd?' and 'How many days are there in six weeks?' The children worked individually, with no need for discussion and no real reason for wanting to know the answers to these questions. They did want to know how many they had got right, but that was all! The same content was approached in a more engaging and useful way by a teacher who set questions as part of an ongoing topic on growth, using the context of human babies. 'Kerry was born on February 2nd. How old will she be on February 7th?' Children made up questions for each other about babies they knew, to practise dealing with days, weeks and months. Questions such as 'David is 9 weeks old. How many months old is he?' gave them the opportunity to discuss whether days, weeks or months are the most appropriate measure to use for a baby's age, and to look at the complexities of calendar months.

There are difficulties as well as advantages in setting mathematical problems for children in real-life contexts, though. A written problem set in a context is likely to require the child to read much more than an abstract question; the teacher may feel that she or he needs considerable background knowledge to be able to set sensible questions; and the teacher needs to be sensitive to equal opportunities issues. None of these difficulties is insurmountable. In particular, it is valuable to use a teaching approach which emphasises practical, talk-based work in small groups or with the whole class, rather than individual work, and which concentrates on problem-solving and investigation rather than finding the right answers (already known by the teacher).

Sometimes it is not a question of searching for suitable contexts, but of making the most of mathematical opportunities which arise from children's interests or in other curriculum areas. For example, work on time and several other aspects of measurement arose from one teacher's observations of children playing at doctors and hospitals in her infant class – including a lively discussion on incubation periods and whether it was a good idea to have 'chickenpox parties', as one child said her mum was planning, 'to get it all over with'. Two children did a mapping diagram to show who might have given chickenpox to whom amongst their friends. A child of seven with a baby sister who was teething drew pairs of clocks showing 'Bonjela times' three hours apart, the minimum period between using anaesthetic cream on the baby's gums. A class of ten year-olds improved their measuring skills by recording 'personal bests' in running, jumping and throwing. Another group of beginner-swimmers, convinced that five metres was an impossibly long distance, was surprised to see how short it was, when chalked on the playground, and compiled a long list of other ways of exercising by travelling five metres.

At secondary level, when maths is taught as a specialist subject, it can be more difficult to make the most of cross-curricular opportunities, but planning with a focus on health can help. Liaison between their maths, science and technology teachers, initially to look at a project on teeth and sugar, resulted in an improvement in work on measurement, record keeping and data handling for year 8 children in one school. They cooked biscuits, experimenting with existing recipes by halving the stipulated amounts of sugar, measuring carefully and recording people's views of the finished products.

Often a starting point which looks at a health issue will also incorporate the cross-curricular themes of citizenship and economic awareness. Children in one city primary school who had been discussing ways of improving the environment around them, decided that the worst problem was dirty pavements caused by dogs and their thoughtless owners. Many of the children were from dog-owning families, and admitted that they were not blameless themselves. A visit from a 'dog warden' convinced them that dogs should use gutters not pavements, and they decided to run a poster campaign to try to convince local dogs and owners to conform.

Groups of children tackled different parts of the project. One group concentrated on deciding what size the posters should be, finding out about A5, A4 and A3 paper sizes and colours, and about printing methods and costs. They asked everyone in the class to question family and friends about what size of poster they would be prepared to put up in their windows. Others collected possible slogans (from adults and older children) and illustrations (from younger children) for the posters, and surveyed opinion about which were most likely to be effective. Should they produce just one poster or would it be better to have a series of four or five different ones? What

Figure 1 Examples of finished posters

would be the best way of distributing them? How many posters would they need? How could they raise the money to pay for them? The project required children to use and apply maths, including measurement, arithmetic, work with money and data handling. Most important of all, the posters were produced and distributed and seemed to have the desired effect in improving the area around the school (see Figure 1, page 76).

Data handling is an aspect of mathematics which can make a very important contribution to health education. In return, health issues are important to the teacher of mathematics, as children are unlikely to see the importance of data handling if they only collect and analyse information which is comparatively trivial, and where the data handling has no practical purpose. Similarly, we do children a disservice if the examples we use in teaching probability are all related to games, and we fail to look at examples where medical uncertainties are expressed using probabilities, for example, in predicting the probability of conceiving a child with cystic fibrosis where both parents are carriers of the defective gene.

Sometimes, data handling may concentrate on increasing children's knowledge of a topic by having them interpret charts, graphs and other diagrams produced by the teacher or outside agencies, looking at topics such as diet, road safety, or the effect of family income on health. In the same way that when young children are learning to write they need plenty of opportunities to read, older children are likely to become more skilful at constructing charts, graphs and diagrams if they are offered considerable experience of 'reading' diagrams produced by other people. They might also sometimes 'rewrite' information to see if they can communicate it more clearly, including acknowledging that diagrams do not always help.

The data handling which forms part of any market research and advertising campaign is an important area to explore with children and young people, particularly to make them aware of the conflict which may arise between the desire of a company to sell its products and the good health of its potential customers. Of course, some advertising campaigns are meant to promote good health; but the planning for many campaigns, whether for commercial or public education reasons, will begin by trying to specify exactly what the important factors are. If you are going to survey opinion or collect information, you first have to agree which questions are the best ones to ask.

A leaflet produced by a Health Trust to try to encourage parents to provide more nutritious packed lunches for their children was examined critically by a group of teenagers whose maths teacher was trying to develop their skills at posing useful questions, and they decided to develop their own leaflet. Initially they just wrote down as many questions as they could think of, then discussed which should be used for a survey. 'Are your packed lunches healthy?' was discarded as being too subjective, while 'Does your packed lunch always include fruit?' was retained. 'Who makes your packed lunch?' (and should, therefore, be the target reader for a leaflet), 'What have you got in your packed lunch today?', 'How much money is the most you could spend per day?', and 'What puts you off trying new foods?' were all agreed to be relevant questions. They supplemented the information gathered by their questionnaire by showing the Health Trust leaflet to a sample group of students and parents, and collecting comments (for example, 'I think the section on cost-cutting ideas is insulting, because it says things like 'margarine is cheaper than butter' and 'fruit is cheaper in the market', as though you wouldn't know that already!').

Hopefully, the next step will be to devise a better campaign, tailored to local needs and promoted by pupils with a strong interest in its success, who have also incidentally increased their own knowledge of the subject. The particular focus of their work could have been almost any health-related topic; it was successful because the teacher introduced a relevant subject as a problem to be considered rather than a set of answers to be learned.

Science

Jennifer Harrison

National Curriculum science has many areas of knowledge and understanding which relate directly to issues of health education. The overlap is considerable and made explicit in *Curriculum Guidance 5*, pp.31–33. Indeed 50% or more of schools who responded to a survey of cross-curricular work in secondary schools (Rowe, 1992), indicated that health education was covered primarily through science, physical education and personal and social education. Health education is, therefore, a very important aspect of science education in that it provides relevance in the form of personal and public matters of hygiene. It gives an opportunity to understand and to clarify personal thinking on health matters. It provides a chance to reflect and to think about evidence in a disciplined way, and finally it provides an opportunity to appreciate that learning about health may involve changes in the way one thinks, explains or does things.

It is important for science teachers to consider the manner of integration of health material. With primary classes opportunities for the direct approach to health topics are numerous, and so classwork on personal hygiene and healthy living can begin by pupils finding out about themselves – how they grow, feed, move, use their senses and about the stages of human development. Ideas about how to keep healthy are gained through the experience of regular exercise and a sensible diet in school, and ideas about how to provide for personal safety are gained by thinking about families and relationships, the use of medicines, and the use of the Green Cross Code. As soon as pupils learn investigative skills and understanding of science in the context of practical explorations and investigations, they begin to appreciate the need for safe and careful practice.

With secondary classes it is more usual to find and incorporate supplementary health material and provide enrichment from within the science lesson. Aspects of health education are to be found in each of the Attainment Targets 1–4, with Sc 2 offering a major contribution in terms of 'life and living processes'. The life processes and the organisation of living things require an understanding of the healthy functioning of the human body, which includes an understanding of how diet, life-style, bacteria and viruses, the abuse of solvents, tobacco, alcohol and other drugs are important influences, and how the body's natural defences can be enhanced by immunisation and medicines.

The physics specialist can exploit the opportunity in the study of light and sound to illustrate the effects of loud sounds on the ear, and relate the hazards of noise and sound levels in the environment to the irreversible destruction of the cochlea in the inner ear. In the context of major human organs there are many examples of technologies used to promote, improve and sustain the quality of life: the various treatments of eye defects lend themselves well to such discussion. Pupils can be alerted to the value of regular NHS eye examinations for the early identification of more serious health problems, or the need for ophthalmic examination in certain occupations (such as laser users). By increasing the pupils' knowledge and understanding of how their bodies work and what they can do to keep themselves healthy the science teacher is raising pupils' awareness of the opportunities for practising preventive medicine. This of course does not lead automatically to the development of high level decision-making skills, but provides the potential for pupils to make informed health choices.

Pupils learn early in their science education of the associated dangers of hot oil, bleach, cleaning agents, and other household materials. When they are older they study the chemical changes involved in the manufacture of materials such as plastics. If they are simultaneously introduced to the energy requirements of the plastics industry and associated social, economic, environmental, health and safety factors, pupils can begin to appreciate that each one of us (and not the scientist alone) is responsible for the health outcomes of such procedures and uses. The study of science clearly has the potential to promote debate on wider social and environmental issues which have a bearing on the health of individuals and communities.

The strategies that are available to science teachers to enrich the science lessons with health-related materials are numerous. One is the use of biographical material such as the story about association of scurvy and vitamin C deficiency (Solomon, 1990). There are also many examples of the practical uses of applied science – such as the flushing lavatory – which have an obvious health context. For older pupils newspaper articles can stimulate discussion on issues like overpopulation or test-tube babies (Wellington, 1993). Indeed the basic principles of inheritance, and their application in the understanding of how some diseases can be inherited, provide the opportunity for important classroom discussion of social and ethical aspects of selective breeding of animals, and controversial issues to do with the correction of human genetic disorders.

There remains, nevertheless, considerable concern that there are aspects of the process of health education which remain uncharted in the science lesson and concern that the potential of science education to contribute to 'the personal development of pupils' (DES, 1989) is often not fulfilled. The reasons for this may be many. I intend now to identify some necessary teaching and learning strategies to bring about successful health education within science lessons.

Health education co-ordinators in school can face particular difficulties in planning. In the *Curriculum Guidance 5* component 'sex education' being able to name the reproductive organs is suggested as appropriate for pupils aged 5–7, whilst knowing the 'basic biology of human reproduction' is appropriate for pupils aged 7–11. This matches the science activities in the parallel key stages, and is supplemented in key stage 3 science by the study of the human life cycle. However, details in key stage 4 science are rather more obscure: 'the study of major organs ... and the consideration of ... the use of hormones to control and promote fertility, growth and development'. Does this really mean a consideration of contraception? *Curriculum Guidance 5* at key stage 4 expects no less than nine associated points of understanding and awareness on sex education, ranging from 'understand Britain's legislation relating to sexual behaviour' to 'recognise and be able to discuss sensitive and controversial issues such as conception, birth, HIV/AIDS, childrearing, abortion and technological developments which involve consideration of attitudes, values, beliefs and morality'. The new arrangements for sex education programmes arising from amendments to the 1993 Education Act are described in Chapter 2. If the school planning indicates that some of these issues (with the exception of HIV/AIDS and other sexually transmitted diseases) are dealt with in the science lesson, then much is expected of the science teacher. At the time of writing schools await guidance from the DFE on the changes to the position of sex education in schools.

What makes for effective sex education has been the subject of debate for many years. An important aspect is the science teacher's ability to find and use the pupils' existing understandings (or misunderstandings) and to show how these conflict with the necessary understanding to grasp the scientific concept – for example, of the menstrual cycle. Research by Phelps (1992) has shown that year 9 pupils know technical vocabulary and are aware of current issues during sex education lessons, but still have poor understanding of many aspects: many were unable to explain where menstrual blood came from; many had an inaccurate geography of the male and female body organs, and the positioning of the ovaries assumed some curious placements (some textbook diagrams are inadequate and several crucial parts of the female anatomy would be better illustrated three-dimensionally using a model, or drawings such as those found in the *Pregnancy Book* [HEA, 1991]). What is also relevant for the science teacher is to be aware of the sort of language that is used to describe sex – its vagueness and ambivalence, its inability to take account of feelings and causes. Pregnant under sixteen year olds tend to describe their state as resulting from 'It just happened'. This is not parallel to the sort of language that is used to explain why one had been knocked down by a lorry when crossing the road. Why is this so? Pupils seem to have little real understanding of their own bodies and sexual issues, including relationships, even though they apparently possess the appropriate terminology. For the science teacher as health educator, ambiguities over terminology can easily arise. Any discussion of 'safer sex' is riddled with obscure scientific terminology, and to use a phrase like 'not exchanging body fluids during sex' is subject to misinterpretation by pupils.

Some of the constraints that exist for science teachers are located in the assumptions that pupils make about the subject. They recognise science as a distinct subject through its specialist setting, often in a laboratory, with its specialist equipment, through the form of its written work, and the inbuilt rules that can govern the sort of talk in the classroom. Teachers control talk to demonstrate what is said or not said according to the expectations of the subject discipline – and the pupils appear to take the rules for granted.

> 'Of particular importance when considering themes are the recognition of rules which govern talk. These are given explicitly or tacitly through the rules of classroom discourse. Teachers at the beginning of the year often tell students what, in general terms, constitutes acceptable talk' (Rowe, 1993, p.5).

Pupils need opportunities through discussion and debate to use the language that they will need to communicate later in their own lives. Such knowledge and experience is powerful; it allows for effective communication about many health issues and for a young person to make informed decisions that will affect their health, happiness and subsequent relationships.

All of this creates a considerable challenge for the science teacher, involving a general commitment to promote health and a specific commitment to teach health issues in a planned way. It may be that not all science teachers are willing or able to deliver aspects of the curriculum in the ways described. Teachers occupy a position of risk particularly when they approach sensitive or controversial issues with pupils. Therefore, health education co-ordinators need to clarify with the whole teaching team just what aspects of delivery can be managed by each teacher, and to examine how they can best be supported. There are teaching skills required in this work which may go well beyond the repertoire of some science teachers, and the skills of talking and active listening when working with pupils in groups are particularly important. Some rules such as including everyone in sharing thoughts, asking for explanations, and probing ideas by asking 'What do you think would happen if ...?' may be helpful. By establishing a non-threatening environment the time for discussion can be fully exploited (Bentley, 1992, p.89).

It is important to relate a subject's principles (the knowledge component) back to everyday life. For instance, legitimising the importance of cervical cancer screening clinics may have to involve a class visit to the clinic and the use of health professionals at such centres. A group of parents and teachers could visit the clinic and help prepare for the class visit. It is fear of the unknown that frequently inhibits young people from seeking advice, and a planned contribution by parents, health professionals and science teachers can allow pupils to make connections between science and everyday life.

References

Bentley, D. and Watts, M. (1992) *Communicating in School Science* Lewes: Falmer Press.

DES (1989) *Non-statutory Guidance to the Science National Curriculum* London: HMSO.

HEA (Health Education Authority) (1991) *Pregnancy Book* London: HEA.

Phelps, F. (1992) 'So you really think you understand sex?' *Education and Health*, **10**, (2), 27–31.

Rowe, G. (1992) *Cross curricular Work in Secondary Schools: A Report to Participating Schools* University of London Institute of Education.

Rowe, G., Aggleton, P. and Whitty, G. (1993) *Subjects and themes in the School Curriculum* (Working paper for ESRC project *Assessing Quality in Cross Curricular Context*) University of London Institute of Education. (permission granted to quote from this paper).

Solomon, J. (ed) (1990) *Discovering the Cure for Scurvy* in *The Nature of Science Series* Hatfield: Association for Science Education.

Wellington, J. (1993) 'Using newspapers in science education', *School Science Review*, **74**, (268), 41–52.

English

Ros McCulloch

Delivering a cross-curricular theme through the medium of a subject always runs the risk that subject considerations will overwhelm and submerge the theme. This is particularly true of subjects with a high level of specificity of content, as Rowe and Whitty (1993) found in their study. On another count they found the success of theme work seriously compromised, for even though the aim of such work is to enable pupils to integrate knowledge and relate it to their own lives 'the onus to make connections between subjects and life experiences seemed to fall mainly onto the pupils themselves'. Arguably, the delivery of health education through the work of the English classroom escapes both charges. First, the protean nature of the subject leaves the teacher free to select the materials used to fulfil National Curriculum requirements; second, individual response and personal growth are so firmly established as valuable elements in the English curriculum that pupils will have many opportunities in their written and oral responses to relate work on health to their own lives, and the lives of their friends and family. The English classroom can thus make a significant contribution to a health education programme that is holistic, and concerned with developing those attitudes and values that will help young people make responsible decisions about their current and future wellbeing. To illustrate this, I shall consider work in language and literature, as well as the part English can play in cross-subject work.

In language work the teacher might use material from the advertising of food and drink. The language and images of glamour, fun and friendship that surround drinks advertisements can be contrasted with the language and images presented in public health advertisements that emphasise the dangers of drink driving and the effects of drunkenness on family life and safety in the home. How effective are these images in encouraging/deterring drinking? How much do our natural tendencies to avoid dwelling on unhappy outcomes, to believe 'it will never happen to us' lead us to ignore the warning material? This discussion can be amplified by statistics on road accidents (especially if age-related), household fires, and figures for personal injury and drink-related illness. Such data can be obtained from newspaper reports or Department of Health publications. The teacher will aim to create a context in which students come to their own conclusions about the consequences of drinking and work out personal guidelines. Another useful area from advertising is to take the pictures of cosiness, family health and harmony, that are used in the promotion of food. Here again pupils can be encouraged to analyse the nutritional as well as the cultural messages being presented. How often is the nuclear family, sitting down to a meal together, the subject of these advertisements? Is this what happens in the pupils' own homes? Does it present a realistic picture of British society today? Perhaps more importantly, the wife and mother is usually seen as taking responsibility for the family's nutrition, choosing low-fat margarine for the husband, heating tasty burgers in the kitchen, popping vitamin-packed fruit juice into the shopping trolley. Pupils might debate whether this passive/dependence model is good for anyone – mother feels guilty if the food isn't eaten, while the rest of the family have no opportunities to learn about nutrition for themselves. They might consider that the equation, food equals love, is particularly insidious. Because people are not seen eating for themselves and for good health then the importance of good eating as a matter of personal responsibility is undermined: if food is seen as a means to the end of gaining affection, then nutritional elements are ultimately trivialised.

After analysing, debating and discussing material like this, pupils can extend their responses in a variety of ways: they can design their own advertisements, construct questionnaires to gauge the effects of advertisements on consumers, prepare oral and written reports on the differences between factual and promotional information, write to food and drinks manufacturers about their advertising policies. Members of a class might work individually or in small groups to produce a portfolio of such responses.

Opportunities for language work across a wide age range also exist in the local environment. Pupils can be encouraged to identify good and bad safety points in their home, at school and in public places. These findings can be presented in public forms as letters, posters, speeches, reports. There is also scope here for personal writing. Pupils can choose a potentially hazardous environment – say a public market, where fruit has been trodden into the ground, stalls are piled precariously high, crowds of people are forced to jostle and push, cars and trucks nose their way through the mêlée. This can give material for a personal account, a piece of narrative fiction, a descriptive piece, or a poem. Pupils can be encouraged to consider the safety aspects of different environments from the point of view of different groups – babies, young children, the elderly and the disabled, as well as the young and able-bodied. Such tasks can be adapted to suit the age and ability of the pupils.

So far, I have touched on knowledge about health education that is fairly easily available to the teacher seeking ways to introduce the topic into English work, and will not call for specialist knowledge in fields outside her competence. There is, however, a very proper hesitancy on the part of teachers to venture into areas of knowledge in which they are not expert, and so it is worth considering ways that the English classroom could be used to co-ordinate and develop specialist, health education-related information gained in other subjects. Work of the sort that has been discussed so far can be extended into substantial cross-curricular projects. Suppose the school has decided to concentrate on a health education project based on the local hospital. Among other things, this could examine links between GPs and patients, numbers of referrals, decisions about priorities, treatment of illness, hospital nutrition, after-care, and the hospital setting as factor in treatment and recovery. A large part of the information-giving, fact-finding school work would be done in mathematics, geography, sociology, psychology, and all aspects of science. What will emerge from this work is that a hospital is constantly making decisions: about priorities for buildings and equipment, about operations, about patient welfare, about fund-raising, and about preventive medicine initiatives in the local community. The English classroom can be the place where the various decisions that the hospital must make are debated: pupils can form hospital committees, can represent various interest groups, and act as local councillors and MPs. Meetings and debates will be conducted in the appropriate modes, with factual information from other subject areas used in oral and written presentations. Freed from the need to provide specialist knowledge the English teacher can concentrate on her main task – the development of pupils' language mastery in speech and writing. Because the hospital decisions will 'have' to be made by the committees, pupils will be involved in attempting to persuade others, resisting the attempts of others to persuade them, and distinguishing fact from rhetoric. In coming to difficult decisions over competing claims, there will have to be negotiation and compromise, which will give pupils valuable opportunities to practise those linguistic skills that are most likely to avoid conflict and lead to consensus. If the school is able to set up links with the hospital the project will have even more salience for the pupils, and the links between the health education work done in school and real life will become more significant.

Of all the resources available to the English teacher in introducing health education into the curriculum, it might be claimed that literature provides the richest source of material. There are situations in narratives that give rise to accidents, whose causes can be examined, and parallels drawn with real life. The significance of patterns of sickness and health in the relationships between characters and the shaping of the narratives can be analysed. However, the power of literature goes much deeper. More than any other subject, literature emphasises the importance of individuals, and, in eliciting an empathic response from pupils, can give meaning and resonance to concepts like 'health', 'sickness', 'relationship', and 'responsibility' that might otherwise seem abstract. Stories about the lives of others, both historical and contemporary, especially in those aspects that bear on health, personal relationships and personal welfare, can have a real impact on pupils. Examples in the literary canon can be taken from the novels of Dickens and the Brontes, while twentieth century books for young people can also provide relevant materials. A good text is Berlie Doherty's *Dear Nobody*, which explores sensitively the reactions and feelings of both the boy and the girl who discover that their relationship has led to her pregnancy. The particularity and specificity of literature allow pupils to identify with the situations presented, and through discussion, to express their own thoughts and feelings. These statements can be self-referential but they do not have to be, for the pupils can speak solely of the events of the story. In this way pupils can, if they wish, explore difficult issues while avoiding the embarrassment of having to express their views in terms of personal experience. This can be important in sensitive personal matters, such as the situation depicted in *Dear Nobody*, or in relationships where there might be other health risks, or where a pupil is dealing with health problems in home life.

Finally, literature makes another, important contribution. Stories usually have a beginning, middle and end. They provide models of how people live through situations, how events have consequences, how people cope with sad occurrences and rejoice at good outcomes. For young people, struggling to make sense of their own lives, living very much in their own present, such models can give advice and support on how they might deal with the health issues and dilemmas they face: coping with illness or bereavement, having regard for one's own health in the face of peer pressure, and facing the responsibilities of relationships with others.

References

Doherty, B. (1991) *Dear Nobody* London: Hamish Hamilton.
Rowe, G. and Whitty, G. (1993) *Times Educational Supplement*, 9 April.

Stories for young people
Swindells, R. (1992) *Tim Kipper* London: Macmillan Children's Books.
Klein, R. (1990) *Came Back to Show You I Could Fly* London: Viking Children's Books.

88

History

David Kerr

The relationship between history and health education is not readily accepted by history teachers. There is no long tradition of links between history and health education in British education as there is with other themes such as EIU and citizenship. History teachers have a narrow conception of health education as the responsibility of other areas of the curriculum notably PSE, science, PE and of other professionals such as the school nurse. This view is compounded by the lack of emphasis in *Curriculum Guidance 5* on the potential links between history and health education (NCC, 1990c). It may explain why health education is one of the least permeated of the cross-curricular themes (Rowe and Whitty, 1993).

If health education is to achieve a whole-school approach then history teachers must take a broader view of health education and be persuaded of its contribution to history teaching. They need, above all, to be convinced of the overlap in aims and purposes between history and health education. The starting-point is teacher recognition of the growth of health education as a significant branch of history over the last 30 years. The history of medicine has attracted a growing band of historians interested in the historical relationship of disease to society (Kiple, 1993; Ranger and Slack, 1992). There is much evidence on the social and economic determinants of health and on how epidemic diseases, from the plague to AIDS, have challenged the stability of every society and shaped our view of disease, medicine and the concept of the 'healthy society'. Health education as history of medicine is a broader, more acceptable, working definition for history teachers. It raises their awareness of the importance of health issues in the curriculum and the use of history of medicine evidence in investigating these issues.

The issues of AIDS, our ageing population, the cost of advances in medical technology and the issue of cost and access to medical treatment, raise many difficult challenges which threaten the stability of society. History is uniquely placed in the curriculum to make a valuable contribution in addressing this broad interpretation of health education in schools and to help pupils to develop the knowledge, understanding and skills which will enable them to participate as 'responsible adults' in meeting these emergent health challenges.

Closer examination of the guidance for health education reveals the overlap with history in the knowledge, understanding, skills and attitudes to be developed and in the approach to learning. The nine components of health education are shot through the programmes of study in history. History offers a unique opportunity to put these components in historical context and help pupils to understand present approaches to them in the light of past experiences in other cultures and periods.

The approach to learning in the guidance document and its aims are familiar to history teachers. Health education is based around the interpretation of evidence and the formation of judgements based on evidence, often concerning controversial issues. The central aim is to help pupils to develop skills and attitudes in handling evidence, in order to clarify their own values, and encourage 'individual responsibility, awareness and informed decision-making' (NCC, 1990c). The goal is to improve their understanding of the roles and responsibilities of the individual and the community concerning health matters and enable them to make more informed choices about health issues. This dovetails with the aim of learning through the Attainment Targets (ATs) in the National Curriculum for history. The overlap is admirably summarised in the guidance for health education for Wales:

History can contribute to health education by:

- providing contexts out of which the components of health education can arise;
- providing historical background to many components of health education;
- developing skills relevant to the broader aspects of school and adult life such as the ability to weigh up evidence and reach a balanced conclusion;
- helping pupils' understanding of motivation and cause and consequence (CCW, 1993).

There is sufficient overlap to suggest that health education can be integrated as part of learning in history in numerous contexts across the key stages. The central question for teachers is how can learning in history help equip pupils with the understanding, skills and attitudes to contribute to 'personal choices and social responsibilities in health to create a healthier future' (WHO, 1984)? It is not enough to assume that pursuing the history ATs will prepare pupils for their choices and responsibilities in health. Successful integration requires history teachers to think through the implications of developing health education as a natural part of the process of learning in history in the classroom.

History can assist best through a process of learning that helps pupils to develop a critical respect for the evidence related to health issues and how that evidence is used. Above all, it includes helping pupils to understand that the concept of the 'healthy society', and the choices and responsibilities of the individual in that society, are ever changing. They should also understand that choices and responsibilities in health are heavily influenced by social, economic and political factors. They should come to appreciate that different interpretations of the concept of the 'healthy society' – *Curriculum Guidance 5* is one such interpretation and *The Health of the Nation*

(Department of Health, 1992) another – in history lead to different questions and alternative ways of seeing things. It requires careful thought and planning in each context. There are a number of steps history teachers might take to develop this process, notably to:

- **identify contexts** in particular areas of history which provide scope for integrating components of health education as part of learning in history;
- **establish lesson intentions and activities** for those areas to help pupils to achieve the ATs in history and appreciate the interrelationship between health issues and social, economic and political determinants;
- **resource** the lessons and identify appropriate teacher interventions for learning;
- **assess** the outcomes in terms of pupil understanding of health issues in modern contexts.

This might be achieved as follows:

Context. The teacher decides that the interwar period in Britain offers the opportunity to investigate social and economic changes and their impact on family life (focusing particularly on the changing role, status and health of women in family life) through the context of the 1920s and the depression of the 1930s. This context can be covered at key stages 2, 3 or 4.

Lesson activities. The teacher designs activities to help pupils to form opinions, from a variety of sources on the 1920s and 1930s (AT3) about the relationship between social and economic changes and the changing role of women in family life and to investigate how interpretations are related to the selection and use of resources (AT2). Pupils are encouraged to compare and contrast those opinions with their views about social and economic changes and the changing role of women in family life in modern Britain.

Resources and teaching. The teacher selects a range of sources showing different interpretations of the impact of social and economic changes on the role of women in family life. The teacher then ascertains pupils' ideas about the impact of social and economic changes on the role of women in the family for these will affect the way pupils will approach the historical context and the evidence presented to them. The teacher turns these ideas back to pupils to enable them to review their own thinking about the impact of social and economic changes on the role of women in the family.

Assessment. The teacher then introduces sources with different views of the impact of social and economic changes on the role of women in the family in modern Britain to ascertain how far pupils are able to transfer the knowledge, understanding and skills developed in the historical context to a modern one.

This is not an easy process to develop and there is no guarantee that pupils will transfer their understanding of the interwar years to question the influences on the role of women in family life in modern Britain. It is vital that that transfer is encouraged if learning in history is to equip pupils with the necessary knowledge, understanding and skills to make informed choices about health issues. It is a learning process which encourages pupils to develop a critical analysis of society and of the concept of health within it. Our rapidly ageing society presents major challenges for future generations in the choices and responsibilities concerning health issues. The health of the world rests on those challenges being met through considered and informed debate. I propose a toast – 'to the future health of the world' – and hope I am still around to see it.

References

Curriculum Council for Wales (1993) *Guidance for Health Education* Cardiff: CCW.

Department of Health (1992) *The Health of the Nation* London: HMSO.

Kiple, K. (ed) (1993) *The Cambridge World History of Human Disease* Cambridge: Cambridge University Press.

Ranger, T. and Slack, P. (ed) (1992) *Epidemics and Ideas: essays on the historical perception of pestilence* Cambridge: Cambridge University Press.

Rowe, G. and Whitty, G. (1993) 'Five themes remain in the shadows', *Times Educational Supplement*, 9 April.

World Health Organisation (1984) *Health Promotion: a discussion document on the concept and principles* Copenhagen: WHO.

Geography

Patrick Bailey

Geography is the study of the world and its peoples considered spatially and environmentally. Some parts of that world are healthier than others; some of its 5.3 billion people enjoy better health than others. People's states of health and un-health powerfully affect their actions and their relationships with others; this is as true of nations as it is of individuals. Because geography attempts to explain human actions, it follows that studies of health and un-health and their causes must be included in geographical research and teaching.

Attempts to account for the distributions and variations of phenomena over the earth's surface, including those of health and un-health, lead into studies of the complicated and finely-balanced relationships which exist between human actions, the conditions and processes of the natural world and the economic, social, political and other environments which human beings generate for themselves. These environmental unravellings show, more often than not, that relationships between the quality and resource endowments of natural environments and the well-being of their inhabitants are extremely indirect. Economic and political considerations commonly intervene, so that some naturally well-endowed areas exhibit wretched living and working conditions (Britain's rich coalfields in the nineteenth century were an example; the Silesian coalfields are another) while areas with difficult environments and few natural resources may achieve extremely high standards of income and well-being. In the modern world, Japan is surely the prime example of such achievement. Its resources consist almost entirely of an ingenious and industrious people and a culture which supports hard work. Since 1945 it has also enjoyed the inestimable advantage of an externally imposed prohibition on armaments. Geography is full of opportunities for exploring relationships between health and other aspects of human activity (see, for example, Mackay, 1993). Some possibilities offered by National Curriculum geography's Attainment Targets (ATs) will now be summarised. These ATs are of two kinds: AT1 deals with skills and supports the other, which deals with geographical information and ideas.

AT1 Geographical skills

The skills particular to geography are mainly those of mapping and the use of other geographical techniques to present and interpret information. In a school course, paper and the computer screen will be used as appropriate to handle geographical materials.

The mapping of information about health and diseases began in Britain with John Snow's demonstration that cholera was transmitted by infected water (Snow, 1855). Snow (1813-58) was a brilliant epidemiologist and a pioneer anaesthetist. At the time of the great cholera outbreaks of 1848-54 he was working in London as a medical practitioner. At that time the way in which cholera was transmitted was still unknown. Snow suspected foul water but he needed to prove it. To do so he mapped the exact locations of cholera cases in part of Soho, also the locations of those who escaped the disease. His map showed dramatically that those who drank from a particular well, into which sewage was seeping, caught cholera, while those who worked in a local brewery and who never drank the water did not. Later Snow extended his surveys to show that Thames water was a major source of infection. Raw sewage was discharged into it; it was also a main source for the city's domestic water supply. Since that time, techniques similar to Snow's have been used with much success to help isolate the causes and methods of transmission of diseases in many parts of the world (see Jarcho, 1970).

A National Curriculum geography course can include the mapping of many kinds of health-related information in the local area, the town, the region. Possible enquiries include the distribution of open spaces in towns which give opportunities for fresh air, exercise and safe places for children to play. Environmental assessment mapping can reveal and quantify variations in healthful and harmful conditions between one street and another, one district and another. Maps of pedestrian and traffic density can show up planning problems and perhaps suggest possible solutions. Heavy concentrations of walkers, cars and lorries in the same streets can be unhealthy, uncomfortable and dangerous.

At the wider scales of country, European Community and world, levels-of-health maps of various kinds can give a very instructive and thoughtful picture of the general well-being (and otherwise) of mankind. Examples of such maps include those which show levels of national income, nutrition, clean water provision; numbers of doctors per thousand of the population; proportion of national income spent on health. Until recently, Ethiopia, one of the world's poorest countries, spent the smallest proportion of its income on health and the largest proportion on armaments of any country in the world. *The New State of the World Atlas* (Kidron and Segal, 1987) is an invaluable source of health-related world maps.

AT2 Aspects of geographical study: places and themes

This second AT first of all tries to ensure that young people gain a systematic knowledge of the world and some understanding of their country's and their own place in it. Links with health education and with other ATs can be made by asking questions about any place being studied such as:

● What conditions make some places healthier than others?

- Are these conditions natural, or are they produced by people?
- Which places and areas are more and less healthy and why?
- How may unhealthy conditions be improved and why is this not always done?

Studies in aspects of physical geography give essential background information about the ways in which the natural world 'works', information which is basic to the understanding of all human activities and their consequences.

Fundamental to the natural world's life-sustaining and health-sustaining processes is the hydrological cycle, the continuous exchange of energy and water between atmosphere, ocean, land and all living things. Every home's water supply and drainage system, however, rudimentary or sophisticated, all farming, all life, depend absolutely upon this cycle. Good health everywhere depends upon keeping this circulating water, this part of the global water supply, unpolluted.

A local survey of water movements on and under the surface, and of actual and possible causes of pollution, is a compelling way of introducing a physical geography unit and it offers many opportunities for health issues to be discussed.

People and environments

Human geography brings in ideas and information about population, levels of urbanisation, migration (and it may be noted that there are more than 20 million enforced migrants and displaced persons in today's world); also about resources and their use, about farming, industry, power supplies, trade and other kinds of exchange. By relating this information to human geography it is possible to construct an 'identikit' of healthy and what may be termed optimistic locations and to compare this ideal model with selected places, near home and further afield.

Studies in environmental geography pull physical and human themes together. They remind us, once again, that the well-being, even the survival of the human race, depends upon our maintaining the health of the paper-thin life-layer at the earth's surface within which we live: the atmosphere, oceans, soils, plants, animals and other living creatures which comprise the biosphere of which we are part. They give opportunities to discuss developments which may upset the fine balances within the life-layer, such as atmospheric pollution and the poisoning of lakes and even whole seas, such as the Black Sea. A less obvious cause for concern, also an excellent topic for study, is the impact of mass tourism based upon the jumbo jet, soon to be superseded by the giant super-jumbo.

David Lodge (1991) has reminded us that 'Tourism is wearing out the planet'. Mass tourism has brought intolerable pressures to bear upon once isolated places and communities, with profound consequences for the health and well-being of individuals and groups. The island of Grand Canary is a case in point. In that small, mountainous island, a huge increase in tourist numbers since 1970 has caused whole new towns to be built in a desert environment, water supplies to be depleted, agriculture to be abandoned, people to move from country to town, usually to find there poor housing, menial work and all too often unemployment. Grand Canary may be healthy for tourists; it certainly is not so for many of its inhabitants, living on the most basic social security in city-edge tower blocks and near-shanty accommodation around Las Palmas.

Conclusion

Despite the problems it brings to light, the geography of health is a hopeful study. It reminds us that health is normal, that everyone could have it. Unfortunately, it also shows us why they do not. It teaches that poverty, bad government, exploitation, greed and war are far more potent causes of unhealth than difficult natural environments. Above all, it is a call to action, an appeal to the young to go out and do more to secure good health for all than their elders have managed to do.

References

Archer, M. (1991) *Aspects of Applied Geography: Development and Health* London: Hodder and Stoughton.

Curriculum Council for Wales (1991) *Geography in the National Curriculum: Non-statutory Guidance for Teachers* Cardiff: CCW.

de la Torre, E., Ayneto, C., Guillen, G. and Perdomo, I. (1990) in *El Turismo* Las Palmas de Gran Canaria: Direccion General de Ordenacion e. Infrastructura Turistica.

DES (1991) *Geography in the National Curriculum* London: DES.

Jarcho, S. (1970) 'Yellow fever, cholera and the beginning of medical cartography', *Journal of the History of Medicine and Allied Sciences, 25,* 131–42.

Kidron, M. and Segal, R. (1987) *The New State of the World Atlas* London: Pan Books.

Lodge, D. (1991) *Paradise News* London: Penguin Books.

Mackay, J. (1993) *The State of Health Atlas* London: Simon and Schuster.

NCC (1991) *Geography: Non-statutory Guidance* York: NCC.

Snow, J. (1855) (2nd edition) *On the Mode of Communication of Cholera* London: Churchill (recommended reading: British Library reference BL 7560 and 67).

Design and Technology

Tina Jarvis

Design and technology as seen by the National Curriculum is the application of knowledge and skills when designing and making good quality products fit for their intended purpose (DES/WO, 1992), using a variety of materials including constructional materials and food to develop artifacts, systems and environments (DES/WO, 1990). This wide approach provides many opportunities to develop health education. Such work can not only entail considering the effect of new machines such as body scanners, artificial ears and endoscopes, it can include studying the production of new drugs, hospital design and setting up organisations for health care in the community. It also involves designing and making relatively small and simple products such as baby alarms, safe toys, suitable meals for expectant mothers, systems for ensuring patients are called for regular dental check-ups and the creation of safe work areas. In addition, the process of evaluating and creating these products helps pupils to recognise that they can take action to promote good health, and introduces them to wider issues where conflicts of interests necessitate individuals making complex, and sometimes uncomfortable decisions, about the provision of health care in society.

Encouraging personal responsibility and action

Design and technology introduces pupils to the process of identifying needs, considering possible action, planning and making products, and evaluating solutions to problems. For example, a group of pupils wishing to respond to the difficulties of an elderly woman with arthritic fingers, might suggest devising a lever arm on taps, a diet sheet based on food known to influence arthritic conditions, ways of brightening up the home environment and a strategy for getting the woman rehoused (Conway, 1990). The advantages and disadvantages of each course of action need to be weighed up, judgements made about what is possible and worth doing, and the success of the final action evaluated. By guiding pupils to make informed judgements, when they leave school they will hopefully continue to consider options in the same balanced way. The general approach of design and technology should also enable pupils to recognise that they are able to improve their life-styles and those of others, including fostering good health.

Promoting good health

There are many opportunities for providing tasks that are within the capability of the pupils and which encourage them to consider the value of different health practices. They could produce a book, video or puppet show covering some aspect of health such as drug abuse, care of old people or a visit to a hospital, or they might make a model clinic or surgery for young children to role play visiting the doctor or dentist. They could also evaluate manufactured products by examining the use and safety of toys, and determine how far different books, videos and equipment help, in their view, to support effective exercise programmes at home.

The use of a wide variety of materials and tools required in design and technology requires teachers to introduce potentially dangerous equipment such as woodwork tools and electrical devices throughout primary and secondary schooling. This enables pupils to learn to act safely with progressively more complex and varied equipment. In addition, as food is one of the materials used in design and technology, issues of diet and healthy eating can be introduced, as well as traditional practices and conflicting information from the media evaluated (Eaton, 1993). Such projects might include challenging the pupils to set up a healthy snack shop; designing and making healthy lunches, sandwiches and snacks; planning a series of family meals; and examining the value and quality of convenience foods.

Evaluating the power of advertising

As part of design and technology pupils are expected to consider the influence of advertising on consumers. By doing so they should become aware of its power and dangers. On the one hand, advertisements can enhance choice by providing information and be used to promote good health care. Consequently pupils could design and produce their own posters and pamphlets encouraging sensible use of alcohol, healthy eating, care of teeth, safe use of electrical equipment, and consideration for others. On the other hand, demand can be created by advertisements in an inappropriate way, as in the promotion of cigarette sales, persuading individuals to follow excessively stringent diets or encouraging the consumption of unhealthy food. As part of evaluation of commercial products pupils should also have the opportunity to discuss these.

Conflicts of interest

There are many issues that pupils will not be able to influence until they are adults, but throughout the secondary school they need to extend their growing ability to weigh up the implications of different courses of action with regard to their own projects, and to consider wider issues in a similarly balanced way.

Technological changes often solve one problem only to create another. Just as the industrial revolution caused great changes in social grouping and family behaviour, so convenience food, improved domestic appliances, and better contraception have lead to the increased freedom of individuals, particularly women, who are now able to use their abilities in many spheres. However, this development may have led to stresses on traditional family structures requiring the need to rethink ways of protecting the well-being of children. Similarly improvements in transport have led to increased lead pollution, thought to damage young children in particular; and refrigeration systems can produce CFCs that are probably damaging the ozone layer, leading to an increase in skin cancer.

Other conflicts arise because of limited resources. Even given excellent technological improvements such as the invention of kidney dialysis machines, plastic hips for replacements and intensive care baby units, there remains, nevertheless, a limited number. Limited money available for health means that choices have to be made regarding which facilities to support. Is one heart transplant more deserving of money than several minor operations? Role play is an effective approach for introducing these issues to pupils. For example, the class might be asked to take the role of a hospital committee which is required to choose four individuals to be given liver transplants from a detailed list of ten dying patients (Hildebrand, 1989).

Other technological developments which have created religious or ethical dilemmas can also be explored through role play, in group discussion or through debates. The class might consider whether life-support machines should be used even though a patient is dying in considerable pain and/or is incapable of a normal life-style. Similar dilemmas have arisen with the extension of biotechnology from the traditional areas of brewing, baking and cheese-making into areas of genetic manipulation, which, although it offers great hope to families with hereditary diseases such as cystic fibrosis and sickle cell anaemia, also leads to many concerns. In a similar way effectively treating infertility is important but many would disagree with the use of human embryos to research into this (Riggs, 1990).

Many other conflicts arise because different individuals, social and cultural groups, organisations, industries and countries have different requirements. The need for an industry to be viable, to ensure that the workers, shareholders and government are protected, can lead to decisions that are not in the interests of all. Only the largest western firms can afford to develop new drugs and even they are reluctant to develop any for diseases that are uncommon in affluent societies. Thus there is little research done on parasitic and other tropical diseases which affect the greatest numbers of people in the world (Perutz, 1987). There may even be pressure on industry to attempt to control the market by removing competitors or to persuade potential customers to change existing more healthy practices, such as encouraging Third World mothers to change from breastfeeding to the use of baby milk powders. When discussing these issues pupils should be encouraged to look for solutions for these problems rather than merely to condone or condemn. Although western organisations do need to consider their practices, great advances could also be made easily and cheaply in the public health of developing countries by teaching people to apply existing knowledge in the control of infectious diseases and improved sanitation (Perutz, 1987). Such discussions might prompt pupils to design ways of delivering basic medication, improving water provision and providing appropriate health information in such locations.

Conclusion

It is important that pupils recognise that technological progress is usually made by a series of small improvements based on evaluating existing situations rather than by major innovations. Consequently they should appreciate that technological change is not the prerogative of 'technocrats' but of all. They should be part of the process, taking action now to protect their own good health rather than relying on uncertain future inventions. An additional value of including health education in design and technology is that such activities provide a social context which has been shown to encourage girls' interest in the subject (APU, 1991; Grant, 1982). In the long term technology will benefit from the different insights into possible innovations that may be provided by women (Bruce, 1986) and those from different cultural backgrounds.

References

APU (Assessment of Performance Unit) (1991) *The Assessment of Performance in Design and Technology* London: SEAC.

Bruce, M. (1986) 'A missing link: women and industrial design' in Cross, A. and McCormick, B. (1986) (eds) *Technology in Schools*, Milton Keynes: Open University Press.

Conway, R. (1990) 'The influence of beliefs and values on technological activities – a challenge to religious education', *British Journal of Religious Education,* **13** (1, Autumn), 49–55.

DES/WO (Department of Education and Science and the Welsh Office) (1990) *Technology in the National Curriculum* London: HMSO.

DES/WO (Department of Education and Science and the Welsh Office) (1992) *Technology for Ages 5 to 16* London: Department for Education and the Welsh Office.

Eaton, R. (1993) 'The use of food in primary design and technology', *Design and Technology Teaching,* **25** (2), 46–48.

Grant, M. (1982) 'Starting-points' in Cross, A. and McCormick, B. (1986) (eds) *Technology in Schools*, Milton Keynes: Open University Press.

Hildebrand, G. (1989) 'The liver transplant committee', *The Australian Science Teachers' Journal,* **35** (3), 70–72.

Perutz, M. (1987) 'The impact of science on society: the challenge for education' in Lewis, J. and Kelly, P. (eds) (1987) *Science and Technology*

100

Education and Future Human Needs, Oxford: Pergamon Press.
Riggs, A. (1990) 'Biotechnology and religious education', *British Journal of Religious Education,* **13** (1, Autumn), 56–64.

Modern Languages

Wasyl Cajkler

> 'The study of a foreign language provides exceptional opportunities for integrating cross-curricular elements naturally' (DES, 1990, 47, 8.2).

While this statement strikes an optimistic note, few practical suggestions to promote positive health emerge from other official documents about the languages curriculum, with the exception of encouraging the idea that pupils might make comparisons between nutritional habits in the UK and those in the target language community. Similarly, recipes are offered as a potential source of discussion and practical activity (DES/WO, 1990, 52).

The non-statutory guidance for the National Curriculum (DES/WO, 1992, 6.7, pp.1–19) identifies the following areas in which modern languages can make a contribution to health education:

personal hygiene routines, eg cleaning teeth;
hygiene products in the home;
food and nutrition, eg diet;
exercise routines;
using helping agencies, eg doctor, dentist, hospital;
safety in the home;
getting on with others.

The areas of experience prescribed in the National Curriculum offer numerous opportunities for inclusion of health promoting activities, for example, Area of Experience A, 'Everyday Activities', could offer opportunities for study of different life-styles and their effects on health; Area B, 'Personal and Social Life', can focus on the health promoting qualities of leisure and recreation activities, with language surveys in the target language of people's engagement in healthy activities.

Where electronic links exist between the school and an institution in the target language community, possibilities exist for the exchange of information on attitudes to health and patterns of health care provision. With greater focus on the European dimension in the curriculum, results from questionnaires administered in partner schools abroad could be entered in a database and analysed not only in modern language lessons but also in other areas of the curriculum.

A focus on health has been a feature of language courses for many years. GCSE syllabuses require basic level candidates to be able to discuss their general state of health, seek help for medical problems, attend to hygiene needs in the foreign language. Students at high levels are expected to describe in detail illnesses and accidents, solve injury or illness-related problems, and buy any necessary medicines or materials. However, the

GCSE has not openly encouraged anything more than this transactional approach to health, seeing it as a further occasion for obtaining services in the target language. While more creative opportunities exist within the GCSE course (notably with the topic of food), examination pressures may lead to these not being as readily exploited as the transactions listed under health and welfare.

However, this may give something of a false impression of recent trends. There has been significant creative effort to include health issues in courses and teaching materials.

Recent mainstream courses, mindful of the statutory requirements for cross-curricular themes, include elements that can easily be exploited for positive health promotion. While publications that post-date the appearance of the National Curriculum are perhaps more explicit in their presentation of the material for its fit to the cross-curricular prescription of the curriculum (for example, Taylor and Edwards, 1992, p.244), earlier courses also offer significant opportunities for health-related language learning activities. *Arc-en-Ciel Books 1* (Miller and Roselman, 1988), *2 and 3* (Miller, 1989) afford a variety of possibilities for interactive activities on finding remedies, promoting health and safety, assuring skin protection, maintaining hygiene and showing social consideration for others. The German course *Zickzack 1* (Goodman-Stephens, 1987) *and 2* (1988) have sections on health, fitness, smoking, drugs, problem-solving and health, and relationships with others. Another book by McNab (1991, p.94, Unit 15) is entitled *Du bist was du ißt* and includes calorie counts, analysis of food for nutritional quality and the study in German of the value of vitamins. McNab and Barrabé (1992, pp.126–145) offer year 7 learners of French a whole unit on health.

This selective glimpse of just a few commonly used texts suggests that mainstream courses have paid increasing attention to health promoting themes and are, therefore, useful sources of materials for meeting cross-curricular requirements (given the appropriate school-wide audit and planning for the health curriculum). Even where courses do not make explicit reference to the requirement, units of text-books include attempts to address health issues, for example, in *Route Nationale Unit 6,* (Briggs, 1992).

At sixth form level, study of health-related issues in the target languages has been common. HIV/AIDS, sex education, sport and fitness, childcare, healthy eating and health promotion (for example, anti-smoking literature, drugs awareness features) have found their way into sixth form studies and course materials (see *Nous Les Français*, Rowlinson, 1987). More recent post-16 course materials seek to maintain this trend (Mort, 1993).

In 1990, NCC envisaged that modern languages courses at key stages 3 and 4 could contribute to a school's relationships, safety, health-related exercise, food and nutrition and personal hygiene (NCC, 1990, p.23). There is evidence that all these issues are being considered (in course books and GCSE courses) with the exception of sex education, which seems to be confined to sixth form studies in the modern language. A Leicestershire school sixth form German class recently engaged in a simulation of a debate about the establishment of an AIDS hospice in a small German village. This proved to be a very successful language learning and general educational experience (Helen Killworth, personal communication) at this level, but is probably impractical and not easily attainable in a large number of key stage 3 and 4 classrooms.

An area in which modern language departments should promote health is in the creation and maintenance of a positive and attractive atmosphere in pleasant and stimulating classrooms (NCC 1990, p.9).

Display of pupils' work, attractively presented and mounted, lifts morale by valuing the co-operative language learning experience. Of course, it is also possible for the foreign language to be used around the school to promote health; in health promotion posters, in safety warnings, on hygiene signs in washrooms. This provides opportunities for reading foreign print in the environment with the added contribution of encouragement of healthy habits. Materials for such display can be made by pupils, as part of their programme of study in health-related areas of experience. In addition, visits to other countries can be used to gather appropriate posters (for example, anti-smoking advice, and warnings about disease such as rabies). The cultural and information sections of the target community's embassy or institute might advise on possible sources for such material.

Modern languages can make a significant contribution in what Spanish educationists might call *educación para la convivencia*, education for living together. The language learning classroom depends for success upon a high level of interaction, communication, mutual support and positive encouragement. The risks to self-esteem are significant in the languages classroom, as pupils are expected to come to terms with an unfamiliar medium. This can be quite threatening, when pupils seek to express themselves in a language in which they have an often limited acquaintance.

Consequently, it is essential that healthy, co-operative atmospheres be fostered; atmospheres that encourage mutual respect and support in the difficult task of learning a language. Following Finocchiaro (1983, p.90) we should:

> 'take steps to help our students from their earliest years to listen to each other with attention and with interest, to appreciate differing points of view, to respect diversity, and to question their own values'.

In short, the languages teacher is an educator as well as language instructor. Teaching materials, course books and recent curriculum developments all support this greater role for the languages specialist. While linguists may be most concerned with communication in the target language, the health of the individual in terms of his/her ability to communicate successfully with fellow human beings will probably not fail as a result of

104

inaccurate grammar or faulty pronunciation. We need to ensure that our children enjoy real communication, accompanied by a feeling of community and real communion between people (Finocchiaro, 1983). In their study of languages, students should be encouraged to interact without rancour, to express opinions and emotions without fear of ridicule, in short to use their language learning for the promotion of their own worth and that of their peers. This represents an enormous contribution to the positive health of the language learner.

References

Briggs, L., Goodman-Stephens, B. and Rogers, P. (1992) *Route Nationale 1* London: Nelson.

DES/WO (1990) *Modern Foreign Languages for Ages 11 to 16 (Proposals of the Secretary of State)* London: HMSO.

DES/WO (1992) *Modern Foreign Languages in the National Curriculum* London: HMSO.

Finocchiaro, M. (1983) 'Teaching for the learner' in Holden, S. (ed) *Focus on the Learner*, London: British Council/Modern English Publications.

Goodman-Stephens, B., Rogers, P. and Briggs, L. (1987) *Zickzack 1* London: Arnold.

Goodman-Stephens, B., Rogers, P. and Briggs, L. (1988) *Zickzack 2* London: Arnold.

Killworth, H. (1993) Unpublished report on *Health Education in Secondary Schools* (University of Leicester PGCE assignment for Professional Course).

McNab, R. (1991) *Lernexpress 2* London: BBC/Longman.

McNab, R. and Barrabé, F. (1992) *Avantage* Oxford: Heinemann.

Miller, A. and Roselman, L. (1988) *Arc-en-Ciel 1* London: Mary Glasgow Publications.

Miller, A. and Roselman, L. (1989) *Arc-en-Ciel 2 and 3* London: Mary Glasgow Publications.

Mort, D., Slack, T. and Hares, R. (1993) *Droit au But* David Murray.

Mort, D., Slack, T. and Hares, R. (1993) *Tout Droit* David Murray.

Rowlinson, W. (1987) *Nous Les Français 1* Oxford: Oxford University Press.

Taylor, G. and Edwards, D. (1992) *Etoiles Teacher's Files 1 and 2* London: BBC/Longman.

Art

Martin Wenham

Health, art and the responsibility of the individual

The decades since the end of the Second World War have seen radical changes in attitudes toward the nature of personal health and responsibility for maintaining it. In the 1950s the very title of the National Health Service (NHS) seemed to imply that the health of the individual is a state which can be maintained (if not actually provided) by others, and particularly by medical intervention through surgery or drugs. A recent television news item gave evidence of one deeply rooted attitude to health care which persists in the community. An habitual and heavy smoker who had been refused heart surgery expressed the view that his inability to give up smoking should not have any effect on his right to treatment, and that – telling phrase – it was the doctors' job to make him well again.

There can be little doubt that in the past the NHS itself has been at least partly responsible, if only by default, for the growth of such attitudes and the health problems of which they are often symptomatic. As recently as 1979, Smith (1979, pp.96–7) remarked that:

> '... the (National Health) service's tendency to underemphasise prevention is notorious ... the majority of doctors and nurses as well as almost all members of other health professions see themselves as primarily engaged in responding ... to the needs of those who are already sick. If all are to play a larger part in prevention there will need to be a change in the climate of professional opinion ...'

Since then there has been a substantial shift of both opinion and practice within the medical profession towards the concept that maintenance of health is primarily the responsibility of the individual, and that medical intervention should be seen as a secondary line of defence when this primary, personal health care fails. This change of emphasis has been reflected in the growth of health education within the community (for example, through the Health Education Authority) and its inclusion in the National Curriculum as a cross-curricular theme.

As *Curriculum Guidance 5* suggests, effective health education is based on: 'encouraging individual responsibility, awareness and informed decision-making'. As I have pointed out elsewhere (Wenham, 1993), art education has a long tradition of encouraging and indeed requiring pupils to learn through a process of thinking for themselves, exercising responsibility for their own work and using their knowledge, skill and experience to make informed decisions. It is this tradition and the values on which it is based, as much as any particular activities or programme, which gives art the potential to make a distinctive and valuable contribution to health education. But before examining some of the ways in which this potential may be realised it will be useful briefly to reappraise some traditional attitudes to art itself.

Art as an investigative activity

From the time of the Ancient Greeks there has been a tendency in western civilisation to regard artists, including writers, musicians and performers, as well as those engaged in the visual arts, as somehow special. The Romantic myth of the artist as one picked out and possessed (perhaps to the point of frenzy) by the gods is perpetuated up to the present day by the habitual use of emotive language in writing about art and artists. Words such as 'creative', 'inspired' and 'expressive' are commonplace, and do a disservice to both art and education because they tend to disguise the fact that, like sound scientific research, most if not all successful art is achieved through a process of investigation and communication. Art and science are often, if not always, much more similar than popular myths and stereotypical images would suggest. If the emotive language is replaced by more neutral terms, a 'creative, inspired and expressive' work of art is seen as the result of an effective and rigorous investigation, which used some good ideas obtained from elsewhere as a starting-point and which communicates ideas, attitudes and emotions to those who interact with it.

Looking upon art as an investigative and exploratory process is likely to make it much easier, particularly for the non-specialist teacher at key stages 1 and 2, to see how it can make a distinctive contribution to all parts of the curriculum, including health education. It has already been suggested that art can make a significant **general** contribution by encouraging personal responsibility and thinking for oneself, thus helping to lay the foundations of responsible action and informed decision-making. But in addition to this there are lines of investigation through which art can promote an understanding of health and selfhood in a much more specific and focussed way, through such themes as one's own individuality, relationships and a visual awareness of one's environment.

Art education and awareness of self

Art is a process of investigation and communication, and it is noticeable throughout history that in spite of a vast range of subject matter, what great artists have investigated most consistently and communicated about most effectively is themselves, their relationships and the ways in which they perceived the world. The close connection between health and one's view of oneself is too well-established to need emphasis here (see, for example, NCC, 1990). As Baelz (1979, p.8) points out:

'Health care is an aspect of human caring, caring for oneself as a

human being with an identity to discover and develop ... Health education is ... the discovery of what we already are ... and the exploration
of what we may become.'

Art education has an essential part to play in the discovery of one's own
identity and communicating about relationships. In the early years, the
drawing and painting of portraits can be used not only to help children
establish a sense of their own individuality, but also to promote the investigation and acceptance of differences and similarities between the
individual and others. The sense of identity and the acceptance of differences can be developed and explored in many ways, but two of the most
useful are through investigations of emotions and dress.

Emotions and their expression can be explored through drawing, painting and sculpture, not only of the face but also of the body, particularly the
hands, while individuality and characterisation can be investigated by
designing (and, if possible, making) masks, make-up and disguises. Such
activities also provide excellent opportunities for relating pupils' own work
to that of other artists, periods of history and cultures.

Dress and costume create opportunities, from the very early years of
schooling onwards, to investigate the relationship between people, activities (including safety aspects) and the world around them. Studies of
variations in the children's own dress in response to the weather or different activities can be carried out in a very wide range of media and extended
to examine a great variety of occupations, climates, personal preferences
and periods of history, with particularly good opportunities for large-scale
and collaborative work. Older pupils can explore their own individuality
and self concepts through designing (and, if they can, making) their own
clothes, personal ornaments and make-up. Here again, the opportunities for
studying other artists, periods and cultures are particularly rich. All these
activities can contribute to health education by helping to develop pupils'
sense of identity and self-esteem; of themselves as uniquely valuable individuals within a social framework of shared values and modes of conduct.

Art, the individual and the environment

Western culture in general, and medicine in particular, has been reluctant to
recognise the importance of the relationship between the individual and the
environment in establishing and maintaining health. As Read (1965) points
out, among many peoples of the world health is a positive concept; much
more than the mere absence of disease or injury. To the Navajo, for example, 'health is symptomatic of a correct relationship between man and his
environment' (Read, 1965, p.5), while our own society provides ample evidence of a negative kind: the mutually reinforcing effects of substandard
housing, homelessness and poor health. As an investigative activity whose
overall aims include the development of visual perception and visual liter-

acy (NCC, 1992), art education has an essential role in developing a sensitive awareness of the environment which any individual must have to remain healthy in the long term.

Just as writing is for many people not so much a means of communication as a way of finding out and clarifying what they think and believe, so for many artists and students art is less a means of representing the environment and communicating one's response to it, and more a way of learning about it through visual investigation. As Paul Klee put it, 'art does not represent the visible: it makes visible'. Only through art activities such as painting, drawing, sculpture and photography can pupils of any age investigate the visual properties of the natural and man-made elements of their environment. The learning brought about through such investigations is essential if they are to develop an understanding of their environment and their place within it.

The development of visual perception and literacy in relation to the environment can begin (Adams and Ward, 1982; Wenham, 1993) in the classroom in the early years, and move out to encompass the whole school, the home and the larger environment which surrounds them. In relation to citizenship, the influence of art in developing environmental awareness centres on responsibility, empowerment, decision-making and constructive change (Wenham, 1993). In relation to health its contribution is perhaps deeper and more subtle. The problem is less that children (or adults) are out of harmony with their environment; rather that most people are unaware that it is an issue which they need to address, let alone one which has significant implications for their health and well-being.

To regard art at its most effective as a rigorous, investigative activity is not to deny the spontaneity and creativity it requires. Rather it is to reaffirm that art and art education are processes of learning which can contribute significantly to a deepening and enrichment of anyone's understanding of themselves, personal and social relations, their environment and the relationship of humankind to it. It is in working to this agenda, so often hidden if not actually disregarded, that art can make its most significant contribution to health and health education.

References

Adams, E. and Ward, D. (1982) *Art and the Built Environment* London: Longman.

Baelz, P.R. (1979) 'Philosophy of health education' in Sutherland, I. (ed) (1979) 20–38.

Edwards, J. and Fogelman, K. (eds) (1993) *Developing Citizenship in the Curriculum* London: David Fulton Publishers.

NCC (1992) *Art in the National Curriculum* London: HMSO.

Read, M. (1965) *Culture, Health and Disease* London: Tavistock.

Smith, E. (1979) 'Health education and the National Health Service' in

109

Sutherland, I. (ed) (1979), 93–112.

Sutherland, I. (ed) (1979) *Health Education: Perspectives and Choices* London: George Allen and Unwin.

Wenham, M. (1993) 'Art' in Edwards, J. and Fogelman, K. (eds) (1993), 70–74.

Physical Education

Angela Wortley

'Mens sana in corpore sano' – Juvenal

Throughout history taking vigorous exercise has been regarded as a major contributor to gaining and maintaining health. Justification for physical education (PE) as a compulsory subject in state schools has always contained key health-related criteria. These have changed over this century and now centre on the illness prevention and health enhancement possibilities to which taking part in regular physical activity can contribute. Most PE practitioners **believe** that health, in terms of improved physiological functioning, positive values and attitudes and enhanced self-esteem can be attained through physical activity. Recent research has provided the evidence that 'fully justifies encouraging participation in physical exercise as part of a national health education programme' (Fentem, Bassey, and Turnbull, 1988).

Health-related-exercise (HRE) has developed throughout the 1980s as a central component of the PE curriculum in most secondary schools. This was prompted by the compelling research findings that supported the crucial role played by exercise in health promotion and illness prevention. During this period many of the initiatives implemented in schools concentrated on the attainment of physical fitness. Practice contained (and continues to include) much individual assessment; fitness improvement was the goal. The Physical Education Association Research Centre based at Exeter University and directed by Dr Neil Armstrong has focused much of its work on issues relating to health and strongly argued for HRE to be included in the statutory orders for physical education in the National Curriculum. Their findings question much of the early practice outlined (Armstrong and Biddle, 1990) but strongly advocate the 'active life-styles' approaches that aim to equip students with a broad range of physical skills and concentrate on participation, not performance.

Health-related aims and objectives are interwoven throughout the statutory orders for PE (NCC, 1992) and can easily be identified within the general requirements for all key stages and in the more detailed specifications for programmes of study. Significantly, HRE objectives are identified separately in the non-statutory guidance of both the NCC (1992) and the Curriculum Council for Wales (1992). The focus within HRE objectives places the notion of health **firmly** within the domain of physiological functioning, particularly cardio-pulmonary efficiency. There is insufficient space here to develop this argument but the selection and isolation of some aspects of knowledge and practice as being health-related might be considered as undervaluing the health-related contribution of other aspects, particularly personal and social development and the enhancement of self-esteem. The holistic view of the person and the total response to exercise is ignored. The physiological emphasis alone is an over-simplistic approach to the multi-dimensional concept of health. The many factors that influence individual behaviour are acknowledged, but generally only in passing, implying they are of little significance or easily tackled. The enormity of the problem of changing individual behaviour is not acknowledged. In terms of pursuing physically active life-styles contributory factors such as heredity, home and family background, peer group pressure and social circumstances are downplayed.

Research projects in Australia, Canada, North America and Great Britain are producing banks of data about the fitness and activity levels of children and adults. At present recommendations based on the data should be treated with caution. Even if obstacles to exercise could be removed, the reality, where many people reject activity because they neither enjoy nor value it, is neatly sidestepped. Too little is known about the nature of the relationship between frequency, intensity and duration of exercise required to bring about health changes. Further research is required to assist teachers in the very difficult task of persuading students of the life-long health 'benefits' possible through active participation. Prominent British exercise science researchers emphasised this need for more evidence and stated:

> 'Exercise will play a part in a population approach to coronary heart disease **only** if the **amount** and **intensity** of exercise needed to confer a decrease in risk are **attainable** and **attractive** for large numbers of people' (my emphases) (Hardman, 1989).

The increasing amount of evidence available to support the possible positive effects of exercise on mental health, personal and social education, improving self-esteem and general well-being is most encouraging. Reading Biddle and Fox (1989), Fox (1991, 1992), Williams (1993) and Underwood and Williams (1991) will give heart to most PE teachers who intuitively believe that participation for its own sake confers health-related benefits. These they articulate in terms such as 'improved quality of life', a 'sense of well-being' and 'feeling good'. Paying more attention to achieving success in domains other than the physical (which concentrates on illness prevention) which can produce responses in the individual in the short term (during and following exercise), and medium and long terms, are more likely to prove attractive to participants. Illness-prevention measures are dependent on establishing life long behaviours (without guarantees of good health) in individuals who may believe they are healthy **without exercising.**

I would recommend reading the contributions of Kirk (1992), Sparkes (1991) and McNamee (1988) to the PE/health education debate. They chart the rise of the 'healthism' movement of the 1980s and question the role of schools in general, and PE in particular, in implementing curricula inspired by this movement. I believe their critiques have had a significant impact on the recent advice to teachers from the health and exercise science professionals. Terms like 'moderate' and 'participation' appear in documentation from the 'healthists' much more frequently with amelioration in advice about the intensity and frequency of exercise needed to achieve health enhancement.

PE/health education resources have followed hard on the heels of the NCC publications. Most resources provide sound practical advice for teachers and schools in addressing the problem of increasing the base level and intensity of exercise taken by school students. Importantly, publications by Sleap and Warburton (1990), Lloyd and Morton (1992) and Sykes and Beaumont (1990) have been developed for primary schools with the non-specialist teacher in mind. Much of the material included has been successfully trialled in schools and provides practical and theoretical advice to enable teachers to implement health education in a health promoting school with particular emphasis on the role of PE. Other resources like *The Exercise Challenge Teacher's Manual* (McGeorge, 1988) are research based and promote the development of HRE objectives more specifically within PE.

National activity/health awareness campaigns in 1993/94 are being sponsored by Persil and Children's World stores aiming to improve participation in young children through school-based schemes. Teachers need to evaluate these developments and select and apply those which fit into their school and departmental health education policies. It is important that short term gains be assessed in relation to their life long curricular objectives.

It is difficult to deny that physical activity can and does play a significant part in enhancing the quality of life of many people. I would go further and suggest that increasing one's level of activity can prolong life and stem the debilitating effects of some diseases of old age, thus improving the individual's quality of life. Promoting active life-styles is central to this process. In the past, success in this area has been limited. Few continue to exercise regularly through adulthood. In working towards increasing the percentage of the population who do maintain healthy, active life-styles the whole school experience has to be scrutinised. Radical changes are needed to increase the number of students leaving secondary education with positive attitudes to exercise. Difficult decisions have to be taken by staff in some schools. There will no longer be the opportunity for kudos to be gained from the activities of a small group of elite athletes, if the exercising climate of the whole community is to be improved.

I would like to put forward these conditions and practices necessary to successfully develop **healthy active life-styles** in students. The following are by no means exclusive:

- maintaining the physical environment to a high level; it should be minimally hygienic and aim to provide a welcoming, pleasant environment conducive to safe, healthy practice;

- involving students in planning the programme at all levels; particularly important is developing an active playground, especially in primary and middle schools, where 'active leisure' can be pursued;
- recognising participation as a **valued** activity in the whole school; this includes planning for, encouraging and rewarding **participation** in activities;
- planning for worthwhile and enjoyable experiences that allow for individual goal setting; to be successful the quality of the teacher–student relationship is crucial in enhancing self-esteem;
- integrating theory and practice of HRE issues; this needs to be done so that students are able to make considered decisions on leaving school;
- using displays to celebrate all types of performers; schools need to eliminate gender bias and identify and include a wide variety of activities, particularly those which are more likely to be carried forward successfully to adult life;
- involving the whole school and local community in fitness and 'taking part' campaigns;
- forging links with the community and local leisure providers and introducing students to local amenities; permanent display areas can be used for disseminating information and advertising local events.

A PE curriculum which takes account of the aspirations, needs and abilities of all students has a realistic chance of success. Until enough evidence is available to determine accurately the differing amounts of exercise needed to confer decreasing risks to health, PE teachers must endeavour to improve the quality of the exercise experience and make exercising more attractive and intrinsically rewarding to more students.

References

Allied Dunbar (1992) *National Fitness Survey: Main Findings* London: Health Education Authority and Sports Council.

Armstrong, N. and Biddle, S. (1992) 'Health-related physical activity in children', *New Directions in Physical Education,* **2**, 71–110, Human Kinetics Publishers (Europe) Ltd.

Biddle, S. and Fox, K. (1989) 'Exercise and health psychology: emerging relationships', *British Journal of Medical Psychology,* **62**, 205–216.

Fentem, P., Bassey, E. and Turnbull, N. (1988) *The New Case for Exercise* London: Health Education Authority and Sports Council.

Fox, K. (1991) 'Physical education and its contribution to health and well-being', *Issues in Physical Education,* 123–138, London: Cassell.

Fox, K. (1992) 'Physical education and the development of self-esteem in children', *New Directions in Physical Education,* **2**, Human Kinetics Publishers (Europe) Ltd.

Hardman, A., Hudson, A., Jones, P. and Norgan, N. (1989) 'Brisk walking and plasma high density lipoprotein cholesterol concentration in previously sedentary women', *British Medical Journal,* **299**, 1204–1205.

Kirk, D. (1992) *Defining Physical Education* Lewes: The Falmer Press.

Lloyd, J. and Morton, R. (1992) *Blueprints: Health Education Key Stage 1* and *Health Education Key Stage 2* (Teachers Resource Books) Cheltenham: Stanley Thornes Ltd.

McGeorge, S. (1988) *The Exercise Challenge: Teacher's Manual* Loughborough University of Technology.

McNamee, M. (1988) 'Health-related fitness and physical education', *British Journal of Physical Education,* **19**, 83-84.

NCC (1992) *Physical Education in the National Curriculum* York: National Curriculum Council.

Sleap, M. and Warburton, P. (1990) *Happy Heart 1: Resources for 4-7 year olds* London: Health Education Authority.

Sleap, M. and Warburton, P. (1990) *Happy Heart 2: Resources for 7-11 year olds* London: Health Education Authority.

Sparkes, A. (1991) 'Alternative visions of health-related fitness: an exploration of problem-setting and its consequences', *Issues in Physical Education,* 204–227.

Sykes, K. and Beaumont, G. (1990) *Exercise and Health: Guidelines for Primary and Middle School Teachers* London: Longman.

Underwood, M. and Williams, A. (1991) 'Personal and social education through gymnastics', *British Journal of Physical Education,* **22**, 15–20.

Williams, E. (1993) 'The contribution of physical education to personal and social development', *Pastoral Care,* **11**, (1), 21–25.

Music

Linda Hargreaves

Music and health education have a great deal to offer each other. Music itself is a therapeutic medium used to relieve stress and create a social atmosphere. Certain types of music can reduce the need for anaesthetic in dental surgery, extend physical stamina in fitness routines, make thriller movies more frightening and increase impulse buying in shops (see Radocy and Boyle, 1988). By integrating health and music education, we can enable children to understand music's influences on the everyday health-related choices they have to make, and provide a **purposeful, real-life context for listening to and appraising music.** This will help many children learn in an otherwise abstract medium. Health education through music is likely to be most effective, however, as part of a whole school health promoting programme, planned by a team of teachers to ensure progression and continuity (King, 1992). As part of such a scheme, music can be brought into the mainstream of the curriculum from its often isolated position at the edge.

Some simple ideas for links between music and health education which can be adapted easily to suit different topics and pupils' ages and stages as required are summarised in the table (see page 116). In the text, we shall concentrate on the **psychological** and **environmental aspects of health education** both of which could be regarded as superordinate components of health education. The remaining seven components provide specific content for them.

Psychological aspects of health education

Music can support this component of health education in three ways:

(1) as a health promoting medium;
(2) as a vehicle for information transmission;
(3) as a source of contentious stereotypes and role models.

Consider, in relation to the last, the role models for girls in music: why are women more likely to become orchestral players than jazz musicians, for example? Pugh (1991) offers some positive examples of women in music.

We shall focus now on how music can contribute to the development of co-operation, self-esteem and the awareness and management of emotions, three strands which underpin all four key stages of the psychological aspects of health.

Co-operation

First, as a health promoting medium, music can exert a direct effect on co-operative behaviour. Fried and Berkowitz (1979) showed that listening to

Health Education	Music AT1 performing and	composing	Music AT2 listening and	appraising
substance use and misuse			Examine the social contexts of music eg parties, relaxation, fun.	Biographical study of jazz musicians eg Charlie Parker.
sex education	Parts of body action songs.			Roles of women in music.
family life education

safety | Sing songs for celebrations birth-days/lullabies. | Compositions about the 'young to old' life-cycle.

Compose jingles for safety slogans. | Listen to world musics used in marriage, death. | Talk about music and emotions in family events. |
health-related exercise	Match musical pattern to movement pattern.	Compose and perform country dance music.	Classify music as calming or stimulating.	Compile tape for a dance/aerobics programme.
food and nutrition	Sing and talk about songs about food.	Compose musical menus of healthy or unhealthy foods.		Analyse music in food adverts.
personal hygiene	New words – old songs eg *Mulberry Bush.*	Compose music for toothpaste advert or rap.		Analyse deodorant, soap or toothpaste adverts.
environmental aspects	Worksongs.	Make sound 'collage' or compose music for contrasting landscapes.	Identify sounds around – garden, street, corridor, home. Analyse TV/film music.	Listen to *La mer, American in Paris* etc and identify musical features which represent the idea or city.
psychological aspects	Simple songs – adapt words to foster self-esteem eg *I'm happy and I know it; I hug myself* (see text).	Compose together in groups: compose self affirmation *ostinati.*	Discuss moods music produces; respect for individuals' feelings; music to manage stress.	Identify composers' ways of creating moods. Roles of women in music.

Table 1 Some activities to link National Curriculum music and health education

Mendelssohn's *Songs Without Words*, which they labelled 'soothing', made pupils significantly more helpful and co-operative than *One o'clock jump* ('stimulative'), John Coltrane's *Meditations* ('aversive') or seven minutes of sitting still with no music. Pupils could classify various musical works along similar dimensions and use selected pieces to enhance the effects of dramatic productions. Second, genuine co-operative groupwork is a regular feature of music sessions. Participants need to listen and respond to each other although they probably need to be taught how to do this. Finally, certain activities using music for information transmission are designed to foster co-operation especially at key stage 1.

Fountain (1990) describes co-operative musical games for four to seven year olds including *Musical Laps,* and *Musical Hugs,* both variants of musical chairs. In another game, *Crowns and Statues,* each child wears a 'crown' (a quoit, or a bean bag) on her head and moves to the music. If the crown falls off, she must freeze and remain a statue until someone replaces the crown for her. Music of varying style, pace, dynamics, pitch and so on, could be used for these games and matched to different types of movement, eg walking, skipping, crawling, thus contributing to the key stage 1 programmes of study for listening and appraising.

FOSTERING SELF-ESTEEM

Whilst genuine co-operative groupwork will in itself promote higher levels of self-esteem (Johnson and Johnson, 1987), songs and activities can be adapted *(I'm happy and I know it)* or selected for this purpose. Older pupils could reword 'nursery' songs, perhaps those that their parents sang, or compose self-affirming songs for a reception year 1 class. Fountain (1990), for example, offers a self-affirming action song to raise self-esteem in key stage 1 children. Entitled *I hug myself 'cause I love me so* and sung to a traditional American tune it begins:

> *Oh I love my knees, and I give them a squeeze,*
> *And I bend them and stretch them as I please.*
> *I love my toes, and I love my nose,*
> *And I wiggle, wiggle, wiggle them until they grow.*

The back, head, feet, shoulders and hips (see sex education, key stage 1 – naming body parts) are included and in a co-operative variation, the children can work in pairs and substitute 'you' and 'your' for 'I' and 'my'.

RECOGNISING HUMAN EMOTIONS

Music affects our emotions. Terwogt and van Grinsven (1991) found that five- and ten-year-olds linked musical extracts to pictures representing 'fear, sadness, happiness or anger' with high levels of consistency. Sloboda

(1991) has found consistent reports of 'shivers down the spine', laughter and 'a lump in the throat' in response to specific pieces of music. The children's responses to music can be a starting-point for the recognition of emotions, their causes and how to cope with them. The stimulative or soothing effects of music are used by therapists to manage clients' emotions, whilst, in some special schools, playing the same music at the same times each day helps children with emotional difficulties to cope with transition times. Much of the research on music and emotion is confined to the use of western classical music, however. Listening to music from different genres and cultures, and comparing and contrasting their emotional responses to it would make pupils more aware of others' emotional responses and of the diversity of cultural expectations.

Environmental aspects of health education

As the success of the Muzak Corporation testifies, music is a powerful medium exploited by advertisers and employers to manipulate our behaviour. Radocy and Boyle (1988) point out how 'rock music of previous decades has been increasingly incorporated into commercials (aimed at) potential buyers in their 30s and 40s'. The key tasks for the key stage 3 music teacher here are to enable children (a) to recognise such manipulative effects and disentangle the musical packaging from the product or message and (b) to select and to compose music which is capable of similar effects on others. The pupils could:

(1) collect and appraise musical extracts from advertisements, films, etc, identify the target audience and analyse the musical elements such as style, pace or instrumentation used to 'hook' this audience;
(2) carry out their own research into the effects of playing different types of music (eg slow or quiet or non-percussive or ... versus fast or loud or percussive or ...) in meeting places or dining areas. They could observe other pupils' behaviour and later carry out structured interviews to find out their responses to the music;
(3) compose, in groups, music for an advert, video or dramatic performance and study its effects on the audience.

Finally, returning to a broader look at cross-curricular links, *Curriculum Guidance 5* links music specifically with hygiene. There are some suggestions for composing and appraising music in advertisements for hygiene products, but one surprising conjunction between the particular musical genre and personal hygiene appears in a rap by De La Soul (1989). It might provide inspiration for some young people:

> *... there's no powder on your odour – That's why **you smell!**
> You might feel a little embarrassed – don't take it too hard,
> And don't make it worse by covering up with some Rightguard!*

Before you even put on your silk shirt and pack your rope,
Just take your big ass to the bathroom and please use a little bit of soap.

References

De La Soul (1989) *Three Feet High and Rising* DLSMCI Big Life Records, England.

Fountain, S. (1990) *Learning Together: Global Education 4 – 7* Cheltenham: Stanley Thornes, in association with the World-Wide Fund for Nature and the Centre for Global Education, York University.

Fried, R. and Berkowitz, L. (1979) 'Music hath charms ... and can influence helpfulness', *Journal of Applied Social Science*, **9**, 199–208.

Johnson, D. and Johnson, R. (1987) *Co-operation and Competition* Hillsdale, NJ: Lawrence Erlbaum.

King, P. (1992) 'Health education in the National Curriculum – all change or as you were?' in Hall, G. (ed) *Themes and Dimensions of the National Curriculum* London: Kogan Page.

Pugh, A. (1991) *Women in Music* Cambridge: Cambridge University Press.

Radocy, R. and Boyle, J. (1988) *Psychological Foundations of Musical Behaviour* (2nd edition) Springfield, Illinois: Charles Thomas.

Sloboda, J. (1991) 'Music structure and emotional response: some empirical findings', *Psychology of Music*, **19**, (2), 110–120.

Terwogt, M. and van Grinsven, F. (1991) 'Musical expression of mood-states', *Psychology of Music*, **19**, (2), 99–109.

Religious Education

Mark Lofthouse

Sex is an arresting word. Sex education as a topic is less exciting. Put sex education in the context of religious and moral beliefs and most teachers, like Sam Goldwyn, are left saying, 'Include me out' (Wragg, 1993, p.72). Given the deep uncertainties within contemporary society concerning sexual values, this reaction is not surprising. Concern about the consequences of sexual permissiveness is fuelling a rising tide of anxiety. This mounting concern is justified by the fact that Britain has the highest rate of teenage pregnancy in western Europe, with 103,000 pregnancies in 1991. In 1992, with political alarm bells ringing as a consequence of these figures, the Department of Health published a white paper, *The Health of the Nation*. A key target in this was to halve the conception rate of under sixteens to no more than 4.8 per 1,000 (Wallace, 1993, pp.1–2) by the year 2000.

The launch of *The Health of the Nation* was accompanied by widespread protests from doctors and health workers concerning the reluctance of teachers to get involved in 'talking to children about sex' (Wallace, 1993, p.1). Apart from what Wragg (1993) eloquently describes as 'the cringe factor', teachers find it difficult to talk to children about sex because society has such differing and often conflicting opinions on the topic. For example, the publication of the Family Planning Association's *Primary School Workbook* (Family Planning Association, 1993) has been greeted with hostility in some quarters. Taking the view that the media drenches children in sexual imagery and innuendo from the earliest age, the Family Planning Association argues that sex education must begin early and needs to be explicit (Hopkins, 1993, p.9). Such explicitness, however, provokes deep anxiety. The Conservative Family Campaign described many of the sex education materials used in schools as 'pornographic'. The Education Secretary, John Patten, expressing his own anxiety about the Family Planning Association's *Primary School Workbook*, went on to declare, 'We are clear that all sex education should take place within a framework which encourages pupils to consider the moral dimensions of their actions'.

This statement brings us to the heart of the matter, to that curriculum territory where the concerns of health and religious education overlap. *Curriculum Guidance 5* sets out in some detail curriculum maps, illustrating where subjects, and in particular Religious Education (RE), can deliver components of health education. The rationale embodied in the approach is that the primary purpose of the health educator is to convey a body of knowledge. The role of the RE teacher is to provide opportunities for pupils to reflect on the facts, and to strain them through the nets of spiritual, moral and belief dimensions. If this is indeed the central objective it needs to be admitted immediately that it has been imperfectly achieved in the past

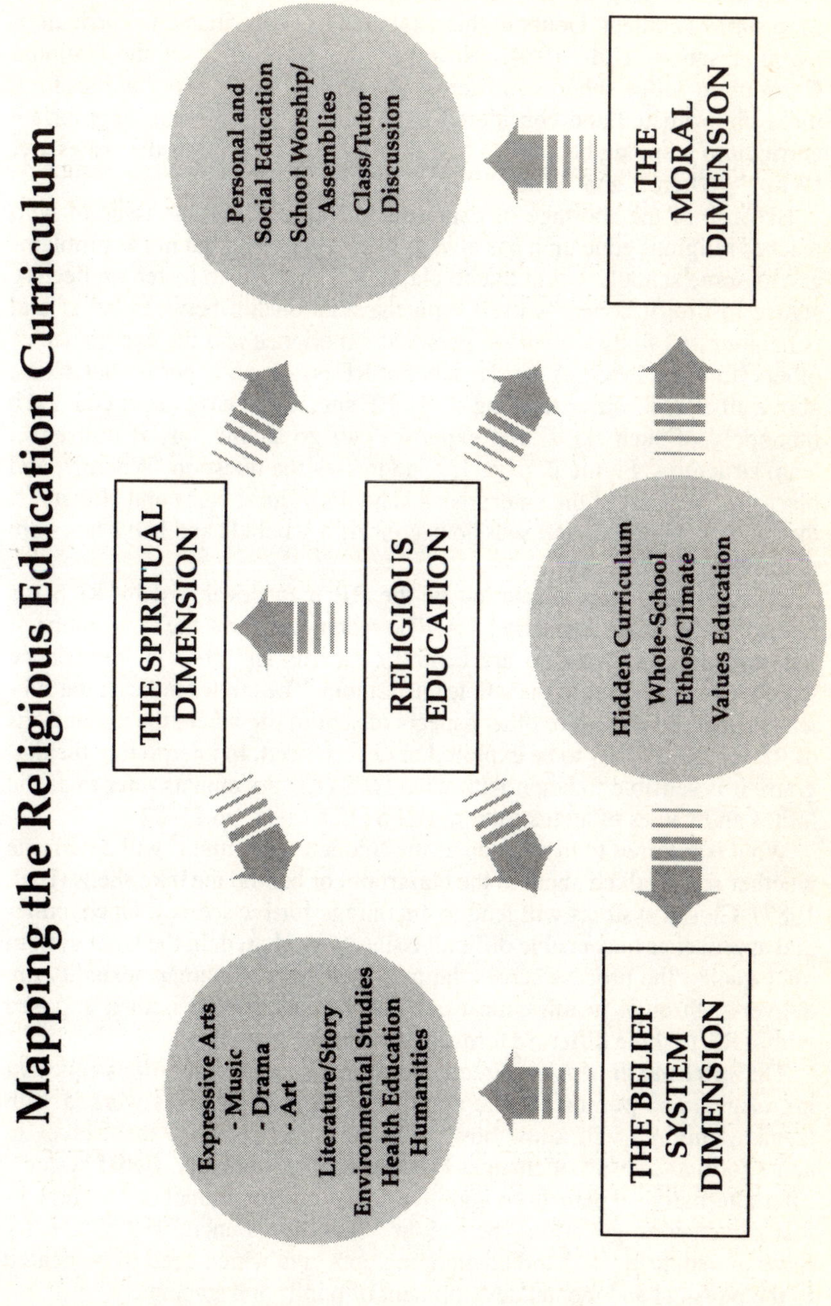

Figure 2 Mapping the religious education curriculum

because of the incoherent development of the two subjects (Goldman, 1964). Both subjects presently suffer from a shortage of specialist teachers (Wilson, 1993, p.1), and this has undoubtedly led to a degree of uncertainty as to subject content. Doubt in this vital area has contributed to curriculum marginalisation (Hull, 1984). However, the embedding of the National Curriculum within schools and across age phases, offers opportunities for a more co-ordinated and considered approach. In this context, appropriate curriculum mapping becomes a first priority. For all schools the issues are, 'Who?' 'Where?' and 'When?'

Because of the shortage of expertise in RE teachers, the issue of who teaches religious education has always been a problem, but not as problematic as some schools would like to claim. RE attempts to foster a reflective stance to life; it concerns itself with the relationship between belief and behaviour and finds a focus on personal experience and the experience of others (Loukes, 1965). A good teacher of RE possesses expertise but needs, above all else, sensitive tutoring skills. RE specialists have never claimed a monopoly of such skills, and expertise can go a long way if utilised in team structures. Figure 2, page 121, addresses the question 'Where?', and places at the heart of the enterprise a school's values, ethos and climate. If these are flawed, shared discussions concerning beliefs and behaviours are unlikely to thrive.

The diagram is an adaptation of the RE map developed by Richards (1992) for Northamptonshire LEA. The rectangles show the dimensions of RE, and these dimensions are central concerns and areas of experience which RE contributes to the whole curriculum. The circles indicate the subjects, curriculum areas or other aspects of school life where the dimensions of RE are most likely to be explored or experienced. In interpreting the diagram, it is sensible to begin with what OFSTED documents refer to as the 'ethos and values of an institution' (OFSTED, 1993, pp.21–22).

What is referred to in the map as the 'hidden curriculum' will determine whether sex is talked about in the classroom or behind the bike sheds (Ball, 1987). Closed systems will tend to encourage furtive secrecy. Open, collegial approaches may enable difficult issues to be shared. In the latter system (and tracing the process across the map) the facts of human sexuality are delivered through health education. The factual content is then exposed within RE to three differing forms of scrutiny.

The **spiritual** dimension directly confronts profound questions concerning origins and purpose of life and death. Anyone who has worked with teenage children will know how such questions can raise themselves in acute form as a result of changes brought about by puberty. **Belief** systems offer alternative explanations and invariably develop **moral** codes and ethical dimensions governing behaviour (Schools Council, 1971). Clearly these are sophisticated and challenging concepts which need to be geared to the physical and mental development of pupils and students.

In tackling the 'When?' issue, teacher judgement is critical. However, a real problem with both sex education and RE is that the time and conditions may never be right. For the reluctant and reticent teacher commercial schemes integrating video and back-up materials may provide a way into the real issues. *Goodbye Peter Pan – A Developmental Sex Education 5–16+* is one of the better curriculum packs available (Brown, 1991). For teachers who like to think their own thoughts and develop their own materials, recent books by Watson (1992) and Astley (1992) provide challenging perspectives on changes taking place within religious education. For teachers in a hurry and needing to integrate RE and health education, the booklet *Sex Education* (Brown, 1993) is concise, accessible and a mine of useful information on agencies working in and across the two areas. Because it has such a high political profile, sex education has been a useful exemplar for tracing through a process. However, teaching health education is likely to ignite a series of potentially controversial processes by confronting issues such as homosexuality, gender differences, drug and child abuse (Hargreaves, 1988, pp.1–6). Further reflection on such issues via moral, spiritual and belief systems, all falling within the RE domain, is an unsettling and disturbing process. In short it is likely to be unpopular, not least because it holds a mirror to the cultural norms and values of the institution.

In the face of such difficulties the temptation to do nothing is powerful. During a recent OFSTED inspection a headteacher, asked to produce his religious education policy, claimed that he could not – because his policy was to have no policy! While a display of such disingenuous pragmatism provokes a degree of grudging admiration, it really won't do. When Pontius Pilate washed his hands he made a policy statement which has reverberated down the centuries just as powerfully as if he had endorsed or countermanded the crucifixion. Doing nothing is not a safe haven.

If inattention, by design or default, is not an option, the thrust of this article is to urge considered action. Clear policies, rigorous curriculum mapping and the creation and application of a process model is an approach offering a potential for coherent action. Clarity of approach breeds confidence, and confidence is the key to gaining involvement and commitment from all concerned. Sam Goldwyn's phrase needs to be reversed so that doctors, health workers, teachers, governors, parents and pupils all say: 'Include us in'.

References

Astley, J and Day, D (eds) (1992) *The Contours of Christian Education* McCrimmion Publishing.

Ball, S. (1987) *The Micro-Politics of the School: Towards a Theory of School Organisation* London: Methuen.

Brown, A. (1993) *Sex Education* London: The National Society for the Church of England.

124

Brown, E. (1991) *Goodbye Peter Pan – a Developmental Sex Education Curriculum 5–16+*. Available from Erica Brown, 7 Elyham, Purley-on-Thames, Pangbourne, Berkshire RG8 SEN (£7.00).

Family Planning Association (1993) *Primary School Workbook* London: Family Planning Association.

Goldman, R. (1964) *Religious Thinking from Childhood to Adolescence* London: Routledge and Kegan Paul.

Hargreaves, A., Baglin, E., Henderson, P., Leeson, P. and Tossell, T. (1988) *Personal and Social Education: Choices and Challenges* Oxford: Basil Blackwell.

Hopkins, D. (1993) 'Start early to fight ignorance', *Times Educational Supplement*, 29 October 1993.

Hull, J. (1984) *Studies in Religion and Education* Lewes: Falmer Press.

Loukes, H. (1965) *New Ground in Christian Education* London: Student Christian Movement Press.

OFSTED (1993) *Handbook for the Inspection of Schools* London: HMSO.

Richards, C. (1992) *A Map of the Religious Education Curriculum* Northamptonshire Local Education Authority.

Schools Council (1971) *Religious Education in Secondary Schools: Working Paper 36* London: Evans/Methuen.

Wallace, W. (1993) 'And baby makes two,' *Times Educational Supplement,* 1 October.

Watson, B. (ed) (1992) *Priorities in Religious Education* Lewes: Falmer Press.

Wilson, K. (1993) *Moral and Spiritual Education* London: National Commission on Education, Briefing Paper No 19 (September).

Wragg, T. (1993) 'No sex please, we're squeamish', *Times Educational Supplement*, November 5.

Addresses

Sex Education Forum: National Children's Bureau, 8 Wakley Street, London EC1V 7QU.

Health Education Authority, Hamilton House, Mabledon Place, London WC1H 9TX.

Social Sciences and Sociology

Tony Lawson

Health Education of the 1980s for the 1990s

The contribution of the social sciences to any programme of health education would seem to be a foregone conclusion. The importance of the
disciplines of economics, politics, psychology and sociology to issues concerning the health of individuals and society as a whole could be
taken-for-granted. Indeed, a cursory glance at the details of *Curriculum
Guidance 5* would suggest that any health education course which
neglected to include a social science component in some way would not be
meeting the requirement of the Education Reform Act 1988 that schools
promote 'the spiritual, cultural, mental and physical development of pupils
at school and of society' (NCC, 1990a). However, the inclusion of seem-
ingly social scientific elements in *Curriculum Guidance 5* is strangely at
odds with the whole thrust of the document, which is founded on an individualistic and not a social view of the purpose of health education.

The emergence of health education as a cross-curricular theme occurred
in the 1980s, when the ideology of individual responsibility was paramount
and the government took direct political control of the curriculum through
the 1988 Education Reform Act. The discourse of health education is,
therefore, informed by an emphasis on individuals and their responsibility
for their own health, rather than the social context within which decisions
about health are made. It is Mrs Thatcher's now famous dictum that 'there
is no such thing as society, only individuals and their families' which provides the context of *Curriculum Guidance 5*, rather than a social scientific
understanding of the factors which may influence health decisions.

The crucial ideological concept implied in *Curriculum Guidance 5* is
empowerment – the emphasis on 'encouraging individual responsibility,
awareness and informed decision-making' (NCC, 1990c, p.7) which is
designed to empower the individual to make healthy choices. The neglect
of the social, economic, psychological and political limitations on individual decision-making in *Curriculum Guidance 5* has the effect of reducing
health matters to moral dilemmas faced by individuals in the carrying out
of their lives. The absence of a perspective which places individual decisions within social, economic and political systems arguably leads to a
programme of health education which is **victim-blaming** in its effects.
Curriculum Guidance 5 can, therefore, be seen as a subtle means of ideological control, which complements the overt political control embodied in
the 1988 Education Reform Act.

This is not to say that there is **no** social dimension to *Curriculum Guidance 5*, but rather that there is a restricted view of the social. The holistic
approach advocated by Tannahill (1990) is not a truly holistic approach, in

that its conception of the social does not go far enough. The emphasis in the document is on health-damaging behaviour' and the 'influence of peer and other social pressures', rather than the 'social and economic determinants of health' referred to earlier in this book, in Chapter 2. It is as if the focus on 'individual's health-related behaviour rather than ... the impact of societal factors on life-style' identified with the 'disease-orientated approach' specified in Chapter 2 has been carried over into the health education of the 1990s. This restricted conception of the social emerges from the Curriculum Guidance itself, where the vague and unsatisfactory concept of 'community' is as far as the social ever gets.

The logic of health education set out in *Curriculum Guidance 5* begins with the relationship between the individual and the family. The school is seen as a means of supporting attitudes and practices conducive to good health, but having 'regard to the relationship between children and their families' (DES, 1986). Where other social dimensions are acknowledged, these are seen in a very restricted way, in terms of social pressures the individual may face, or the 'overlapping interests of individual, group or community health' (NCC, 1990c, p.3). But the notion of community employed here is a very narrow one, referring to the environment surrounding the school, leisure facilities, parents and welfare and health services. In a world where the globalisation of economies and cultures is significant, this emphasis on the local community can only be a part of the story.

Tina McGrath has pointed out the difficulties in such an individualistically based approach when she argues that 'making an impact on behaviour patterns conditioned by years of imitating elders and now reinforced by expensively funded commercial advertising, is quite different from trying to improve knowledge or skills, the traditional aims of the education system' (McGrath, 1989). However, *Curriculum Guidance 5* is based on a self-empowerment approach rather than a radical approach, as defined by Tones (1981). So, while the aim may be to improve children's abilities to control their own lives, *Curriculum Guidance 5* does not address adequately the social environment in which those choices have to be made.

In the nine components of a Health Education Curriculum 5–16 (NCC, 1990c, pp.4ff), the possibility for a social scientific input can be charted fairly easily. However, the nine components, identified in the document, themselves encompass the individualistic thrust of the *Curriculum Guidance 5*, from personal hygiene to sex education. Nevertheless, there are obvious ways in which the social sciences can contribute to the nine components. As might be expected, the social scientific input increases as the pupils move through the key stages and as they become more able to deal with social and political issues in a reasoned way.

So, in key stage 1, the only overtly social scientific input concerns **family life education** and the requirement that pupils 'know that there are different types of family and be able to describe the roles of individuals within the family' (NCC, 1990c, p.12). Key stage 2 builds on this aspect and also introduces a real psychological dimension in looking at the **psychological aspects of health education**. Key stage 3 introduces several social scientific strands, from concepts such as stereotyping, child development and maturation, to political issues, such as legislation and the National Health Service. By key stage 4, there is a consistent thread of social scientific concerns running through all nine components, from understanding 'how political, social, economic ... decisions affect health' (NCC, 1990c, p.20) in **environmental aspects of health education** to the 'importance of legislation affecting the workplace' (NCC, 1990c, p.19) in **safety**.

It is relatively easy to criticise individual items of the nine components and indeed this has been done. For example, Brown reports on the dangers of gender-stereotyping in the **family life education** component (Brown, 1992). The dangers of a lack of a social science dimension to health education have been highlighted in various materials produced to assist its delivery. In the workshop activities produced by the Health Education Authority, reference to 'Man's role in society' (HEA, 1990, p.428) highlights the necessity for social scientists to be involved in health education matters.

But a more deep-rooted problem must be the lack of a satisfactory social scientific context. *Curriculum Guidance 5* pays lip service to the social, but it raises more questions than it answers. As a minimum, the following problems emerge from the conception of the social which is employed: How can the issue of smoking be dealt with, without reference to the power of tobacco industries? How can sexuality be comprehensively covered, without a consideration of the restrictions on discussion implicit in clause 28 of the Local Government Act (1988)? How can physical exercise be encouraged with no acknowledgement of the issue of access? How can the whole area of health and illness be examined with only a minimal reference to the NHS (NCC, 1990c, p.17)? How can the influence of poverty on diet be reduced to a vague reference to 'financial influences' (NCC, 1990c, p.19)? It is the lack of the dimension of social, political, economic and institutional power which distorts the discourse of health education and prevents the real empowerment of the individual.

It has already been documented that little use has been made of the social sciences in health education (Charlesworth, 1991) in pre-16 schooling. Yet the need for a properly social scientific input to health education is particularly important in the post-16 sector where the social sciences are strongest, because it contains those students who are legally entitled to engage in 'risk-taking behaviour' (Hill, 1987). The alternative to a health education programme informed by the social sciences may be to fall back on the 'shock horror' tactics criticised by Dyson (1993). Schools should be providing students with a comprehensive social understanding of health issues, so that real choices can be made and individuals empowered to take

128

the social and political action which may be necessary to promote health.

References

Brown, T. (1992) 'CG5: The good, the bad and the guidance', *Education and Health*, **10** (1).

Charlesworth, D. (1991) 'Health education: from policy to practice', *Education and Health*, **9** (2).

DES (1986) *Curriculum Matters 6: Health Education from 5 to 16* London: HMSO.

Dyson, S. (1993) 'An end to shocking education?' *Social Science Teacher*, **22** (2).

Hill, F. (1987) *Health Education 16–19: Health Action Pack: Background Papers* London: Health Education Authority.

HEA (1990) *Exploring Health Education* London: Macmillan.

McGrath, T. (1989) 'What is 'good practice' in health education?' *Education and Health*, **7** (4).

Tannahill, A. (1990) 'Health education and health promotion', *Health Education Journal*, **49** (4).

Tones, B.K. (1981) 'Health education: prevention or subversion?' *Journal of the Royal Society of Health*, **3** (2).

CHAPTER 7

Equal Opportunities in Health Education

Special Educational Needs

Sylvia McNamara

To address the issues concerning health education confronting students who have special needs, their teachers, parents and carers, it is important to define what we mean by health education. The content areas are clearly outlined in *Curriculum Guidance 5* and include growth and development, personal development, grooming and presentation, self-esteem, keeping healthy, keeping safe and sex education. These are all areas that could be taught to students with even quite severe special needs. The guidance makes clear that the aims of health education are to 'help pupils make informed choices, establish a healthy life-style and build up a system of values', as well as providing information. Thus decision-making as a skill needs to be taught.

At first there may seem to be a problem of resourcing for students who have been identified as having 'special educational needs'. These needs (as every mainstream class teacher and every special school teacher will know) are wide and varied. The issue of resources is, in fact, more easily resolved than other problems, and can be overcome by the kinds of imaginative adaptations at which teachers are so skilled (see Coombes and Iqbal, 1993).

The most difficult problem is the extent to which students with special needs can make decisions for themselves. This problem is not just a cognitive one but it is also attitudinal. For students with special needs (whether they are placed in mainstream primary or secondary schools, in special schools or units, in residential or day settings) the biggest problem faced, in terms of an entitlement curriculum or equality of opportunity for access to the education component of the National Curriculum, is the attitude of adults. There still seem to be educators who question the rights and abilities of students with special needs – their right to 'normal' relationships and a social life, and their ability to make good sense of information and make decisions for themselves.

There is also the paradox that despite misgivings about their own ability to do so, it is even more important for teachers of students with special needs to address the issues of sex education and substance abuse than for mainstream teachers. This is because the parents of students with special needs not only feel the embarrassment that other parents often feel, but also seem to experience shock at the idea of their children becoming mature sexual beings with strong emotions of their own (Jupp, 1992). Both Craft (1991) and Dixon (1992) have produced good resources on sex education for teachers of students with learning difficulties, for example, on the use of diagrams, drawings, dolls and puppets. However, Craft highlighted at a recent conference (Iqbal, 1993) that as yet there is no vocabulary in British sign language or its derivative, Makaton, for certain parts of the body or for words such as 'hurt' or 'pain'.

The crucial issue in mainstream schools is classroom climate, and the extent to which students with special needs have been included. If no work on 'working in groups' has been done – such as: random pair and random groupwork; discussing how it feels to be left out; devising group rules; using 'including statements' when participating in groups; discussing friendships – students with special needs are likely to have experienced rejecting behaviour from their peers and be feeling too low in self-esteem to participate in potentially embarrassing or threatening discussions. For examples of this type of work see Hopson and Scally, 1981; McNamara and Moreton, 1993; TACADE, 1990; Johnson and Johnson, 1987.

It was for this reason that a disability pack was written by Moon (TACADE, 1992). It includes a number of ideas for helping primary children to explore their feelings about disability. These ideas can be adapted for both secondary and special school settings. Once a climate is established in the mainstream classroom, where all children, including those with special needs, feel confident to express their feelings, it is then possible to work through the processes of health education as outlined in *Skills for the Primary School Child* (TACADE, 1990). This is a carefully graded pack, containing National Curriculum-related activities, to address the themes of: myself; building self confidence; growing and changing; people I love; listening well; communicating well; negotiation skills; assertion skills and making mistakes. Also addressed are the kinds of skills children need in order both to communicate well with one another on sensitive issues and to make healthy life-style decisions.

The pack of supplementary lesson cards (TACADE, 1993) addresses the cross-curricular themes. Section one examines: eating, exercise, drugs, smoking and alcohol. Section two examines: sex, conception and birth, and HIV/AIDS. The skills approach is taken as a methodology in the TACADE work: this means that students with special needs can work at a rate that suits them and on particular skills – those needed to identify themselves, their families and to share with others their feelings about themselves, those needed to communicate, to listen, to respond; those needed to talk about their own feelings; those required to be assertive and to set goals.

The philosophical platform of the *Skills for the Primary School Child* pack is that raising of self-esteem is crucial in helping children to make good choices in the area of health education. One of the main advantages for a child with special educational needs in the mainstream classroom is the potential for good examples. In the special school setting the only people behaving in socially acceptable ways tend to be the adults. In the mainstream class there are many peers who can model correct behaviour, eg taking turns in group discussion, sharing in simulation exercises, stating feelings in certain exercises. Peers can also 'cue in' the student with special needs by saying things like 'What do you think Dipack?' or 'You haven't said much, Emily'. They can also provide appropriate feedback:

'You're dribbling again, David, so use your hanky'.
'I can't hear you, say that again more slowly, Jamie'.
'I don't like it when you punch me, Lucy. Just ask me for help'.

Provided that a good ethos has been established, it is possible for children with special needs to improve their self-esteem and, therefore, be in a good position to make decisions about health-related matters. In special schools where peer modelling and feedback is absent, it is much harder but more crucially important for teachers to help their students form positive self-esteem. In her manual on sex education for students with severe learning difficulties, Craft (1991) has written a section on sociosexual skills, which starts with a unit on self-esteem. For her, also, self-esteem is an important component in decision-making. There are exercises to help students explore appropriate behaviour with peers, family members, close friends and in more formal situations. Her reasoning is that students with severe learning difficulties may well have developed, and in some cases even been 'allowed or encouraged to continue, inappropriate childish behaviour long after childhood'. Such inappropriate behaviours mean not only that the students may end up in unsafe situations but also are likely to be ridiculed by peers without special needs. Such ridicule damages self-esteem.

When dealing with issues of sex education the major stumbling block for students with special needs is the attitude and skills of adults and associated problems of communication. The difficulty of teaching vocabulary and concepts to students with both severe and profound learning difficulties has been imaginatively addressed in *Image In Action* (1993) with creative combined use of drama, puppetry and active learning techniques to explore effective ways of teaching health and sex education. The new drama programme *Dragon's Breath* (Ward, 1993) is another useful resource for initiating a lively discussion amongst students with moderate or severe learning difficulties. A similar point can be made about drug education. Michell (1993) found that secondary students with special needs, who often have emotional and behavioural difficulties, had a 'significantly higher smoking rate than other groups' and 'were the heaviest smokers', and 'for most schools smoking as a health issue is not very high on the

132

agenda'. Clearly in order for students with special needs to have equality of opportunity in the area of health education, time and money has to be given to training and resources. It is only when the adults who support these special young people develop the necessary positive attitudes, policies and teaching programmes that the benefits will be seen.

References

Coombes, G. and Iqbal, S. (1993) *Special Needs Health Guidelines* Birmingham LEA Guidelines.

Craft, A. (1991) *Living Your Life* Wisbech: Learning Development Aids.

Dixon, H. (1992) *Chance to Choose: sexuality and relationship education for people with learning difficulties* Wisbech: Learning Development Aids.

Hopson and Scally (1981) *Lifeskills Teaching* London: McGraw Hill.

Image In Action (1993) *Information Pack* from Image In Action, Jackson's Lane Centre, Archway Road, London N6 5AA.

Iqbal, S. (November 1993) *Balancing the Act* A joint conference of the National Association of Special Education and Birmingham Health Education Unit.

Johnson, D. and Johnson, R. (1987) *Learning Together and Alone: Co-operation, Competition, and Individualisation* Englewood Cliffs, NJ: Prentice Hall.

Jupp, K. *Everyone Belongs: Mainstream Education for Children with Severe Learning Difficulties* London: Souvenir Press.

McNamara, S. and Moreton, G. (1993) *Teaching Special Needs: Strategies and Activities for Children in the Primary Classroom* London: David Fulton Publishers.

Michell, L. (1993) 'A special need to smoke,' *British Journal of Special Needs*, **20** (2), 44–47.

TACADE (1990) *Skills for the Primary School Child* Salford: TACADE.

TACADE (1992) *Understanding Disability* Salford: TACADE.

TACADE (1993) *Skills for the Primary School Child–Part 2* Salford: TACADE.

Ward, C. (1993) *The Dragon's Breath* (Theatre in Education production on smoking and health for ages 7–13), Birmingham LEA Health Education Unit.

Gender Issues

Mel Vlaeminke

> 'A secondary school version (of a booklet about food) should ... provide ideas for bachelor cooking courses so that boys are not left out' (Holmes, 1985, p.128).

> 'Women's own likes and those of their children are set aside in order to ensure that those of their husbands are catered for' (Charles and Kerr, 1986, p.60).

These two quotations, taken from reputable recent books on health education, together highlight two of the key arguments which this section intends to explore:

(1) The experiences and expectations of girls and boys, in terms of the practical organisation of their lives, present and future, are likely to be significantly different. It is, therefore, unhelpful to treat both sexes in the same way.
(2) Power relations between the sexes permeate every aspect of our lives and most crucially, the nature of relationships between the two. Strategies which aim to promote individual decision-making, self-esteem and personal control have to be considered in this light.

The difficulties inherent in these statements add up to a formidable burden for health educators.

To consider the food issue a little more fully, many would object to the sentiments expressed in the first quotation; the unwritten implications for women are too depressing. One begins to wonder how far things have moved from Victorian times, when Sophie Bryant, one of the pioneering headmistresses of late nineteenth century England stated, 'the chief function of women is the making of the home and the preservation of the social side of society' (Bryant, 1895, p.100). Yet it is probably a true reflection of the division of labour in the majority of households occupied by both females and males. It is possible, therefore, for the health educator – as for career teachers and other kinds of educators – to argue that it is more useful to prepare youngsters for the lives they are realistically likely to lead, than to instil in them a dissatisfaction with circumstances shaped by factors far beyond their influence or control.

The objection to this approach is that, in accepting the status quo, it helps to perpetuate stereotypes, which are limiting and demeaning – in the case of gender, to both sexes. In the example under discussion, there is a basic injustice associated with expecting females to do much of the domestic work needed to sustain life, yet denying them the control needed to make effective decisions, even within that sphere. But that is exactly what the authors of the second quotation which heads this section, found from their research into family diet. Men (of all socio-economic classes) favoured a traditional meat and veg or fried meal, they were generally resistant to 'healthier eating', and they could be hurtfully direct in expressing their preferences. Women were often content to accept and rationalise this state of affairs, thereby suppressing their own tastes and their knowledge of nutrition. As these researchers concluded, 'the message is clear that targeting women alone with health education will only serve to increase their burden of guilt rather than lead to a transformation of family eating habits' (Charles and Kerr, 1986, p.72).

This really does point up the range of meanings of the word 'responsibility'. Consider the difference between 'holding a position of responsibility', with its implications of status and power, and 'carrying the responsibility for ...', as an unavoidable and burdensome task. 'Responsibility' is a common word in the new methodologies in health education, with their encouragement of approaches which enhance 'individual responsibility' and 'informed decision-making' (NCC, 1990c). If the individuals concerned are constrained by cultural or societal pressures from exercising that responsibility or executing those decisions, then one questions how much is likely to be achieved.

No programme of effective health education can hope to succeed without being able to anticipate with some confidence how the participants are likely to be affected. When engaged in role plays or simulations or group discussions, do girls and boys speak honestly, listen respectfully and support each other? We don't really know, because no-one has analysed such activities in the field of health education, where relations between the sexes are a major part of the agenda as well as part of the method. It is generally known, however, that two-thirds of all divorces are initiated by women; their most common complaint is that their husbands don't listen to them. And we know that in other group learning situations, females and males function differently. Boys are more demanding of teacher time, more competitive and impatient, they interrupt girls more and are dismissive of girls' opinions and abilities. They have a higher opinion of their own performance than objective tests justify (ie high self-esteem), while girls have a lower one (ie low self-esteem) (Stanworth, 1983; Whyld, 1983). These are manifestations of the cultural norms which dictate that males do not show anxiety or distress, do not express their feelings, do not concede arguments or control of discussions, and do not reveal signs of 'weakness' or 'effeminacy'. Yet it is striking how repeatedly the term 'young people' is employed in the literature of health education, as if they were all the same. A few nods are made in the direction of multiculturalism, but gender differences hardly figure at all.

We also have evidence of a statistical nature to show that girls and boys respond differently to programmes of health education and subsequently perceive different needs and anxieties. For example, less than half of 16-19 year old males discussed sex with their parents and only 6% with any sort of health professional; overwhelmingly their knowledge and opinions were derived from discussions within their own male peer group (HEA/MORI, 1990; Allen, 1987). Thus 'macho male' culture is readily perpetuated, along with the unattractive vocabulary of sexual relations. Mahony (1985, p.45) refers to the 200 + ways to abuse women verbally, many of which could be readily listed by schoolgirls. What has also been described is 'the double standard of sexual morality' – the 'slag' or 'drag' dilemma which encourages 'both boys and girls to categorise girls in sexual terms, whereas boys do not define each other in the same way' (Lees, 1987, pp.146–7). The same verdict is expressed in a recent analysis of women's experiences of the supposed sexual revolution of the last 30 years:

> 'In truth, there was almost no change in the way men related to women sexually, other than to welcome women's greater availability ... The sexual revolution had failed to shift that stubborn and all-pervasive icon of sexuality in our society, the young girl' (Linda Grant writing about her book in *The Guardian*, 24 September 1993).

This all adds up to a formidable challenge for any young person trying to shape their own attitudes and values. Males and females both say they would welcome more opportunity to talk to each other about sex and other health education matters (Allen, 1987), but, for the reasons outlined above, providing this is not a trivial undertaking. While health educators cannot be expected to grapple with the whole business of sexual politics in society, they cannot, it seems to me, do their job if they fail to acknowledge – and act upon – the gender dynamics associated with communication, self-esteem, peer group norms and personal decision-making. It isn't enough to 'have a discussion' in the sense of filling the time with words. It requires practical experience of counselling skills and small group management to ensure the atmosphere of unusually high trust and mutual regard which genuinely honest communication demands. All of us need help and practice in developing good communication skills, especially adolescents and especially boys. There is a persuasive argument for boys-only groups at an initial stage in acquiring these skills, preferably led by a skilled male teacher – and there's another problem! Single sex groups can also be used periodically to rehearse preconceptions and doubts about particular issues, before bringing girls and boys together.

Such approaches may require new skills and understandings amongst the adults concerned, and fairly complicated arrangements at the organisational level. But if health education is to contribute as much as it can to the development of equal opportunities, it has to capitalise on its unique access to the nature of relations between the sexes. It is difficult to see any other way by which teenagers can move away from the stereotypical roles and language which breed exploitation and low self-esteem and deny equality.

136

References

Allen, I. (1987) *Education in Sex and Personal Relationships* London: The Policy Studies Institute.

Bryant, S. (1895) 'The curriculum of a girls' school' in *Special Reports on Educational Subjects Vol 2*, Education Department.

Charles, N. and Kerr, M. 'Issues of responsibility and control in the feeding of families' in Rodmell, S. and Watt A. (eds) (1986) *The Politics of Health Education*, London: Routledge and Kegan Paul.

Grant, L. (1993) *Sexing the Millenium* London: Harper Collins.

HEA/MORI (1990) *Young Adults Health and Life-style: Sexual Behaviour* London: HEA.

Holmes, M. 'The multicultural background to health education' in Campbell, G. (ed) (1985) *New Directions in Health Education*, Lewes: Falmer Press.

Lees, S. (1987) 'The structure of sex–gender relations: implications for sex education' in Campbell, G. (ed) *Health Education Youth and Community*, Lewes: Falmer Press.

Mahony, P. (1985) *Schools for the Boys?* London: Hutchinson.

Stanworth, M. (1983) *Gender and Schooling* London: Hutchinson.

Whyld, J. (1983) *Sexism in the Secondary Curriculum* London: Harper and Rowe.

Developing Health Education in and for a Multicultural Society

Pauline Hoyle

Many issues of relevance to the promotion of good quality health education are similar to those promoting education for equality. Equality education enables the learner to develop to full potential and ensures appropriate access to the curriculum and the learning environment. This requires that account is taken of the whole person and how different starting-points, ideas and experiences influence learning. Therefore, in equality education all aspects of the person, the physical, social, cultural, emotional and intellectual, must be considered.

Health educators are concerned with the promotion of quality of life – including the physical, social, emotional and mental well-being of the individual. For equality to permeate health education, the intellectual or knowledge aspects of the curriculum need to be entwined with the emotional or affective dimensions and dealt with simultaneously. For example, in teaching about smoking, pupils need to know not only about the effect of smoking on breathing, but also to consider the social and/or emotional reasons for smoking.

For health education to offer appropriate access and fully develop the potential of all learners, account needs to be taken of all factors influencing the person and their learning such as the learner's gender, cultural background, ethnic group and class.

It is useful to define what is meant by culture in order to consider how it is important in health education:

> 'A culture is a way of life and may encompass the notion of life-styles as well as that of high culture, ie that which is held by the dominant or educated groups to be desirable pattern of life, or set of tenets by which one aspires to live. It may also include the ideas of social status that one achieves or hopes to achieve through education and/or socialisation. It is often, but not always associated with language or religion. For instance, it is possible for one to be English and lead an Islamic cultural life ... The concept is too broad and cultures too dynamic to be accurate as a means of classifying peoples. However, curricula may involve a selection from culture or cultures and may, therefore, be aptly described as multi-cultural' (Hussey, 1982).

It is useful to compare this with Hussey's definition of ethnicity.

> 'Ethnicity is the term used to denote the ideas of a group to which one belongs through self identification or identification by others. The skin colour, type of hair and physical features common to a group may

be the means of identification. Some ethnic groups may be identified by language ... some by religion or country of origin, others by both language and region of country of origin ... yet others by religion, language and culture.'

Therefore, for health educators to promote equality they need to consider how the ethnicity or culture of a person may be part of their emotional or affective dimension. A health curriculum that promotes equality must ensure that the emotional or affective dimension of the curriculum takes account of the learners' culture and/or ethnicity.

To deliver a health education curriculum which enmeshes the cognitive and the affective a variety of teaching and learning approaches is necessary. The NCC suggests that a range of learning opportunities should be available for pupils, which includes assessing evidence, solving problems, making decisions, holding discussions and so on. These have implications for the teaching approaches adopted and the management of the classroom. In addition equality educators suggest that learners bring a range of ideas, experiences and attitudes to the learning situation depending on their culture and/or ethnicity. This means that the approach to the curriculum, what and how it is taught and the environment in which it is taught must be adapted so that it is accessible to each and every learner. The teaching and learning approaches adopted, therefore, must enable pupils to develop trust and clarify their values while taking account of their cultural and/or ethnic needs in learning.

Health education is not only about giving people knowledge about various aspects of health but also enabling them to have skills and understanding of the issues so that choices and informed decisions can be made. Religion, ethnicity and/or cultural values influence decisions.

Lessons need to take into account not only beliefs of the teacher, but also of pupils; for example, many religious groups have rules and protocol about various foods; Catholics fast and avoid meat on special religious days, Muslims and Jewish people avoid eating pork, Hindus avoid beef and there are requirements for the preparation of food such as Halal or Kosher practices. Some of these customs may have evolved for scientific reasons such as the hygiene of pork under certain feeding conditions as well as for religious reasons. Other practices such as veganism in non-Hindus maybe influenced by social, political or economic concerns. Teachers who are aware of their pupils' background (cultural, ethnic and religious) and use appropriate teaching and learning strategies will enable pupils to acknowledge and build upon their experiences. Only in this way can young people be supported, not undermined, in their cultural identities.

Racism can have negative results. When pupils are subject to covert or overt racism within a school their self-esteem is affected and their decision-making ability impaired. The opportunity for constructive value clarification is lessened. Pupils experiencing racism or prejudice may counter the racism by rejecting their cultural or ethnic background in order to conform to expected racist societal norms. Obviously this is a whole school issue and will affect all aspects of pupils' achievement as well as their access to the health curriculum.

The following paragraphs illustrate how equality education can be addressed by some of the nine components in *Curriculum Guidance 5*. Pupils are very interested in and aware of the current practices of drug taking, and the effect of drug taking on the body is included in the science National Curriculum. However, this area of the curriculum could be expanded to suggest the historical, social and political context of cocaine taking, for example, the use of cocaine in the places where it is grown such as China, Thailand and Pakistan. Historically, it is also well documented that in Britain in the last century many affluent people, as well as poets, authors and painters, took cocaine. It was socially acceptable and until very recently you could still buy at Harrods a gold pocket case which had a mirror, cutting implement and a place to store cocaine. Tracing the use of such drugs and linking it to the current trends in drug taking can be of interest to pupils. In order to ensure aspects of equality pupils would need to be able to consider the importance to the economy of many developing countries of growing opium and the affect on the farmers and their families if growing of opium ceased.

Another example of how the delivery of the health-related curriculum could be treated to include issues of equality is to be found in the components environment aspects of health education, and food and nutrition. Pupils are often asked to analyse their food consumption in terms of a balanced diet and energy intake. This could include a consideration of consumption and production of chocolate bars. The consumption of chocolate in the UK is very high. All the cocoa and some of the sugar used is imported. The study of the amount of energy required to make a chocolate bar could include transporting the products to the UK and comparing this with the energy output from eating a bar. Aspects of environment education could be considered through the study of: the cash crops of cocoa and sugar and the effect of cultivation on both local environment and the economy of local people; international trade in primary products and associated influences on the economics of developing countries; industrial processing of foodstuffs and influences on nutrition and value.

In addressing sex and family life education, issues of equality are important. The different practices that occur across cultural groups, and the role of women in child rearing, are issues which need addressing in these areas. For example, circumcision occurs in many cultures throughout the world and is sometimes viewed as an important rite of passage in a boy's development. There are both social and health reasons for this practice. However, female infibulation (sometimes referred to as female circumcision) occurs only in few cultures and particular social groups. This practice, perpetrated by men, has no health advantage, and is clearly a result of the subordinate position of women.

The psychological aspects of health education could include issues of equality in several ways. Modern western medicine, or allopathic medicine, is very tied to the use of drugs produced by drug companies and is considered the norm in many countries. However, this medicine is relatively new and the drugs have only been available in large quantities in the last fifty years. Homeopathic medicine has been relegated and considered unscientific by some people. A study of this area could include examining historical methods of healing such as the extent and application of knowledge that healers, many of whom were women, had and still have in many societies. The past and the present use of homeopathic medicine could be compared with the current use of allopathic medicine by doctors (who, as the considered experts, have control over what treatment or which drugs might be prescribed or administered).

The shortage of appropriate teaching resources is sometimes cited as a difficulty for teachers trying to develop such approaches. There are sources available but teachers may need to adapt them for use in a particular context. The Association for Science Education (ASE) has produced *Science and Technology in Society* materials (SATIS) for teachers and pupils, and a useful package of INSET materials (Thorp, 1991). It is important that each subject within the whole curriculum works within a framework of equality. A list of general principles (Watts, 1987, p.19), which promote equal opportunities in science education, includes the following:

- incorporate a global perspective;
- understand issues relating to justice and equality;
- elaborate science in its social, political and economic context;
- make apparent the distribution of and access to power;
- make all people involved in science overt and not hidden;
- incorporate a historical perspective;
- start from and value the experience and knowledge of children;
- use flexible teaching and learning strategies and give emphasis to the learning of science;
- integrate practical approaches with the work as a whole.

These principles have relevance across the curriculum.

In summary it is possible for health education to approach issues of equality, and in particular issues of race equality, through ensuring that the affective and the cognitive dimensions of the curriculum are presented simultaneously. This can be achieved by using teaching and learning approaches which: acknowledge the whole person and the person's background; enable pupils to make informed decisions (see, for example, Thomson, 1993). The context of the delivery of the curriculum needs to ensure the inclusion of the issues of justice and equality, discussion of the distribution of power, and a perspective that encompasses the social, economic, political, historical and global background.

References

Association for Science Education (ASE) (1986) *Science and Technology in Society* (SATIS) Hatfield: ASE.

Hussey, M. (1982) 'Education in multiethnic society', *Multiethnic Education Review*, **1** (2), 6–7.

Thomson, R. (ed) (1993) *Religion, Ethnicity, Sex Education: Exploring the Issues* London: Sex Education Forum/National Children's Bureau.

Thorpe, S. (ed) (1991) *Race, Equality and Science Teaching, an active INSET manual for teachers and educators* Hatfield: Association for Science Education.

Watts, S. (1987) 'Approaches to curriculum development from both an anti-racist and multicultural perspective' in *Better Science/ Secondary Science Curriculum Review – Working for a Multicultural Society,* compiled by Ditchfield, C., London: Heinemann Educational/ASE.

CHAPTER 8

The Role of the Community in Health Education

The Health Professionals

Alison Timmins

The involvement of health professionals in schools began at the turn of the century as the public health movement gained momentum and legislation was introduced to improve the health of the population. School doctors and nurses were appointed whose key functions were to undertake statutory medical examinations, promote hygiene and advise on infection control. Early medical examinations revealed appalling levels of ill-health in the school age population (Baly, 1985).

Since then the health of school children has improved dramatically as better sanitation and improved housing conditions and nutrition have taken effect. While the early detection of health needs remains an important part of the current health service there is an increasing emphasis on the promotion of health within the school community (HVA, 1991). The term 'school community' is a broad term encompassing not only the formal curriculum but also the rather more subtle aspects such as the physical and social environment and links with the wider community.

While the key health professionals working within schools are the school nurse and school doctor (BPA, 1992), there are increasingly important links with other community based health professionals such as general practitioners and health visitors.

There are a number of ways in which health professionals can have a positive impact on health within the school community. These are briefly outlined in the following section. In the second section are two short case studies of interesting initiatives which have been undertaken within Leicestershire.

The Contribution of Health Professionals

DEVELOPING SCHOOL HEALTH POLICIES

Many schools are taking a much broader view of health than merely ensuring that a planned programme of health education takes place. Such 'health promoting schools' are concerned with the creation of healthy environments geared towards making healthy choices the easier choices (SHEG, 1990).

Policies may range from a whole policy for health or may focus on specific issues such as an anti-bullying policy or promoting the school as a 'smoke-free' environment. School nurses, in particular, are frequently involved in working closely with schools in the development of such policies to which they bring their knowledge of the feeder schools and the local community. They also provide important links with other health professionals such as dietitians whose expertise may be required in, for example, the development of a healthy eating policy.

Collaborative work also takes place in the ongoing monitoring and review of health-related policies to ensure their continuing relevance to the health issues in the school.

PLANNING HEALTH EDUCATION PROGRAMMES

Health professionals can play an important role in working alongside teaching colleagues in planning effective programmes of health education across the curriculum.

The *My Body Project* (Health Education Council, 1983), for example, is well established within Leicestershire and has been used effectively with year 4 children to improve their knowledge and practical health skills such as tooth brushing. In one school the project was jointly planned and evaluated by the teacher and school nurse and the shared responsibility and opportunities to explore each other's roles were seen as key gains from the project (Leicestershire Education Authority, 1993).

INFORMAL HEALTH PROMOTION

School nurses and doctors are frequently involved in providing advice and support on a range of health issues to staff and pupils within the school. Within many secondary schools 'drop-in' sessions have been established in which the school nurse is available for informal discussion. These contacts have often led to further involvement as problems such as eating disorders or sexual health concerns emerge.

HEALTH PROMOTION CAMPAIGNS

There are many opportunities for health professionals to play a key role in contributing to campaigns organised at both national and local levels. A recent example was the 'Play it Safe' campaign promoting safety which was held in a number of schools involving joint planning between teachers, health visitors, school nurses, health promotion officers and members of the local community.

Two Case Studies

Case Study One: Developing School Asthma Policies

Healthy Leicestershire – A Plan for Health (LHA, 1993) identified asthma as one of the key programme areas for health improvement. A number of objectives were defined including action on improving the detection of asthma sufferers, reducing associated environmental factors and managing asthma effectively.

In order to focus these objectives specifically on the school setting, one of the school nurses has worked closely with the schools for which she is responsible and has developed locally agreed school asthma policies.

The process of developing an asthma policy involves a number of stages including:

(1) liaising with the school staff and governors and organising a parental survey to identify children with asthma;
(2) developing programmes of asthma education for parents, teachers and governors;
(3) negotiating a policy which is based on research and which covers the following aspects:
    (a) parental support and involvement;
    (b) access to inhalers;
    (c) sport and exercise;
    (d) environmental factors (eg a 'smoke-free' school);
    (e) the management of asthma attacks;
(4) launching the policy by distributing details to parents of children with asthma along with an asthma record card (developed by the National Asthma Campaign) to be completed by the general practitioner;
(5) collating asthma record cards which are maintained as an active register by close liaison between parents, school staff, school nurse, school doctor and the primary health care team.

This initiative has been warmly welcomed by parents, teachers and governors and has demystified much of the fear surrounding the management of asthma in schools. Developing closer links with the primary health care team has enhanced continuity of care from the home to the school setting.

Case Study Two: The 'Happy Apple' Project

The 'Happy Apple' project aims to involve everyone in the school community in moving towards making healthier food choices. It was developed by the Leicestershire Education Catering Services in conjunction with the Leicestershire Nutrition and Dietetic Service and has been used successfully in many primary and middle schools across the county. One of the key features of the project is its multidisciplinary focus involving joint planning between teachers, school nurses, school cooks, dietitians, pupils and parents. The project is based on a simple system of colour coding foods (fats, for example, are 'red' while fruit is 'green') so that an easy assessment of a balanced diet can be made. This case study outlines the way in which the project was undertaken in a large county middle school.

Preliminary meetings were held involving the headteacher, school nurse, dietitian, school cook and a representative from the school meals services. The commitment from each member of the planning team was crucial in determining the success of the project. It was agreed that the project would run for two weeks in which there would be an emphasis across the school on eating a balanced diet. The following activities were undertaken:

(1) In the week prior to the launch of the project the school nurse and dietitian met with each of the classes during registration and publicised the 'Happy Apple' project.
(2) The school menus were reviewed for the project period and some changes were agreed including the availability of a salad bar. The dietitian colour coded the menus so that everyone had clear information on the foods which they were choosing.
(3) A school newsletter was sent to parents in which the project featured prominently and parents were invited to school for lunch during the project period. Pupils who normally took packed lunches were also invited to participate in the project.
(4) A competition was launched in which pupils were invited to have their meals assessed by the school nurse and dietitian. Those who had made healthy choices were awarded a 'Happy Apple' sticker. The house with the highest number of stickers won the 'Happy Apple' award.
(5) During the project classroom activities focused on raising awareness of healthy eating and physical exercise. Teaching plans were developed collaboratively between teachers, dietitian and school nurse and there was an emphasis on improving pupils' decision-making skills.
(6) The local press attended the school during the project and publicised the event in the local community.

In order to evaluate the project each pupil was given a simple questionnaire to complete. The results indicated that the project had a positive impact in terms of increased knowledge and skills in this area. The salad bar continued beyond the project period as a result of its popularity. One of the key gains, however, was the involvement of the whole school community in this health promoting initiative.

ACKNOWLEDGEMENT

I am particularly grateful for many helpful discussions with the school nurses of Fosse Health Trust in the preparation of this chapter.

146

References

Baly, M. (1985) 'The setting' in Nash, W., Thruston, M. and Baly, M. (eds) *Health at School,* London: Heinemann Nursing.

British Paediatric Association (1987) *The School Health Services* London: BPA.

Health Education Council (1983) *My Body Project* London: Heinemann Educational.

Health Visitors Association (HVA) (1991) *Project Health: Health Promotion and the Role of the School Nurse in the School Community* London: HVA.

Leicestershire Education Authority (1993) *Working Together For Health: Guidelines for Schools and Colleges* Leicestershire County Council.

Leicestershire Health Authority (1993) *Healthy Leicestershire – A Plan For Health, Consultative Document* LHA.

Scottish Health Education Group/Scottish Consultative Council on the Curriculum (1990) *Promoting Good Health* Edinburgh: SHEG.

Address

National Asthma Campaign, Providence House, Providence Place, London N1 0NT.

The Role of Health Promotion

Marilyn Stephens and Hugh Graham

Concepts and definitions

Health promotion is an important and vital feature of the public health movement. It has emerged during the 1990s as a concept which has brought together what were often seen as disparate fields of study. Health promotion can be identified as a key element of the health services of most western countries and, through the offices of the World Health Organisation (WHO), many emerging countries also.

Health promotion has always been dependent upon and inter-dependent with the public health movement (MacDonald and Bunton, 1993). As an emerging discipline, health promotion has become increasingly broader in its range, drawing as it does on the alliances that are necessary for health gain (Department of Health, 1992).

Definitions of health promotion abound. For the purposes of this contribution, the WHO (1984) definition '... health promotion is the process of enabling people to increase control over and to improve their health ...' will be used. Whilst expressed simply, nevertheless, this wording best expresses a way forward. Until recently health promotion has relied very heavily upon the dissemination of health information, targeting health messages at the public in the expectation that this would somehow bring about the desired changes in people's life-styles. It has become increasingly evident that to be effective, information campaigns should not take place in isolation; that they must be combined with a variety of other activities. Health promotion has become a multifaceted exercise which includes education, training, research, legislation, policy co-ordination and community development.

This article utilises a concept which portrays health as a part of everyday living, an essential dimension in the quality of all of our lives. Health is envisaged as a resource which gives people the ability to manage or even change their surroundings. It is a concept which emphasises the role of individuals and communities in defining and redefining what health means to them.

Characterised as it is by diversity, it has to be recognised that definitions of health promotion used by any one organisation will be influenced by the social context of that organisation (MacDonald and Bunton, 1993). A universal definition might be almost impossible, and it may be preferable to allow a certain elasticity of definition (Simpson and Isaac, 1982). Definitions of health promotion could then represent issues to do with health promotion goals (target populations) as well as the focus and type of intervention (Rootman, 1985). It follows, therefore, that promoting better health can no longer be seen as the prerogative of health professionals; it must involve the population as a whole including politicians and administrators and challenge the traditional knowledge-orientated programme so often found in schools and colleges.

In summary, the term health promotion represents a major change in the way that improved health is now perceived (McQueen, 1989) and involves legislation, provision of services, marketing methods, use of the media and education. Greater emphasis has been placed on identifying barriers to health and adopting strategies to remove these so that individual and community life-styles can be improved (Ashton and Seymour, 1988).

Health Promotion Departments

Health promotion departments are mostly, but not exclusively, funded by the National Health Service and can be found by reference to the local health authority. Both the size of a health promotion department and the number of staff employed therein may vary across the country: their function, however, remains constant and, since the publication of *The Health of the Nation* (Department of Health, 1992), has been endorsed by central government as well as local authority. Health promotion departments (and the East Sussex department in particular), will have common identifiable aims:

(1) to increase public awareness of issues that affect health;
(2) to encourage and enable people to value their health and lead healthy life-styles;
(3) to assist in the creation of services and social environmental conditions which help to maintain health.

The range of activities in which a department such as East Sussex might engage in order to pursue such aims are considerable and varied. The supply of publications and publicity materials on a wide variety of health issues is an important function; the free loan of a range of audio-visual resources is equally crucial. The provision of training and the presentation of displays and exhibitions are often linked to a national campaign, sponsored usually by the Health Education Authority or the Department of Health. Most important of all is the relationship between any health promotion department and other agencies who are concerned with promoting better health. Whilst the practical roots of health promotion departments lie primarily in the National Health Service, the academic roots for the philosophy of health promotion lie in what might be called the primary feeder disciplines – psychology, education, epidemiology and sociology.

Education is, of course, a much older field of study than health promotion. For a variety of reasons, however, not least that many of those currently working in health promotion came to their careers through training to be and practising as teachers, educational theory and practice have always shaped health promotion in fundamental ways. Some of the controversies within health promotion have their antecedents in educational discourse. It has been suggested that the two fundamental aims of education are to increase autonomy on the one hand and to initiate learners into knowledge on the other (Weir, 1993) and that both aims are compatible with health promotion. To be autonomous is to be free, to be in control of one's own life, and to be able to make decisions without coercion or fear (Peters, 1966). Accordingly the WHO claims there is no conflict between the goal of autonomy in education and the goal of health promotion, as the goal of health promotion is to empower people to make their own decisions about health. Whilst rhetoric such as this falls easily from the lips, the practice is neither easy nor usually comfortable. The logical consequence of accepting autonomy as a goal for the health promoter is to agree that if educated people choose to act in an unhealthy way then, provided it does not impinge on the freedom of others, this must be seen as an acceptable end result of an educational process (Tones, 1981). Some people working in health promotion would find it very hard to feel satisfied with such an outcome.

The purpose of these opening paragraphs has been, therefore, to attempt an outline of the context within which health promotion departments find themselves in their relationship with the education world. The relationship between the East Sussex Health Authority and the East Sussex County Council Education Department, which will form the subject matter of the remainder of this article, will exemplify elements of the above and should be seen as a case study set in that context.

The East Sussex Educational Response

In East Sussex, in the late 1980s, curriculum support for health education was led by three advisory teachers, funded by the East Sussex County Council. Liaison with the health districts at this time helped shape policies and clarify priorities. The upgrading of Personal Health and Social Education (PHSE) in 1990 making one post a county adviser for PHSE (with inspectorial duties) was reinforced by the arrival of a new Chief Education Officer with commitment and experience in the development of PHSE.

During 1991/92, this team of three set up central courses and school-based work mainly in the primary phase. A successful and well documented model of training was in place by September 1992 with just under 50% of primary schools and 80% of special (day) schools having received some input. Of secondary schools 42% had also sent one or more representatives to central courses, mainly about HIV/AIDS. From April 1991–1993 all courses were funded in total by the education authority with some support from social services and the health authority, and all were oversubscribed.

Funding from HIV/AIDS monies was provided for a sexual health project for two years to support all phases of education, including the Youth

Service, in the development of a more effective sex education curriculum. Three new advisory teachers were appointed to join the existing PHSE team. These members were funded exclusively by the East Sussex Health Authority but managed by Education, enabling a particularly effective partnership with teachers, lecturers and youth workers. The project is guided by a steering committee with representatives from the health districts. The expansion of the team enabled both an extension of the scope of the work and more concentrated development. This work has included:

- the production of sex education guidelines for the advisory service;
- the production of playground packs to facilitate the implementation of hygiene procedures;
- enabling schools to focus their approach to hygiene procedures;
- assisting the primary schools to examine their sex education policy statements;
- continuing to provide an on-going governor training programme;
- continuing to provide a variety of INSET programmes for staff in primary and secondary schools;
- developing peer education programmes in a variety of settings;
- working with parents;
- working with young people in various contexts;
- contributing to multi-agency work in both the statutory and voluntary sector.

This work is informed by local networks and data, national surveys and trends and, of course, by national guidelines such as *Curriculum Guidance 5*. Government circulars and Education Acts also make considerable impact. In East Sussex, the health authority funded the local collation and analysis of a nationally used questionnaire (Balding, 1993). Encouraged by the county adviser for PHSE 64% of schools took part, yielding important and current data for many agencies associated with young people and their families. Success is measured in terms of processes and outcomes with respect to policies for sex education in schools and youth clubs and developed programmes and schemes of work for PHSE. The team looks for:

- increase in quantity and quality of school-based sex education policy documents;
- an improvement in the depth and quality of sex education received by children and young people;
- attendance at and evaluation of courses;
- increase in the number of effective sex education programmes;
- self reporting of teachers (in terms of confidence, knowledge, awareness).

These indicators of success are compatible with goals for health promotion expressed earlier in this section, such as autonomy and empowerment. The relationship between health and education in East Sussex is enhanced as much by being based on shared concepts about processes and outcomes as on financial expedients. Funding remains a central issue as posts are still short term (limiting effectiveness and long term planning) and financial support for central courses is vital if attendance (with cover in schools) is to remain high. Currently advisory teachers for sexual health can offer their services free, unlike most other advisory teachers and advisers. Funding and constructive support from the health authority has enabled an already successful team to expand and become an invaluable county-wide resource for teachers and youth workers in personal, health and social education.

References

Ashton, J. and Seymour, H. (1988) *The New Public Health* Milton Keynes: Open University Press.

Balding, J. (1993) *Health-related Behaviour and Young People* Exeter University.

Department of Health (1992) *Health of the Nation* London: HMSO.

MacDonald, G. and Bunton, R. (1992) *Health Promotion Disciplines and Diversity* London: Routledge and Kegan Paul.

McQueen, D. (1989) 'Thoughts on the ideological origins of health promotion' *Health Promotion,* **4** (4) 339–342.

Peters, R. (1966) *Ethics and Education* London: Allen and Unwin.

Rootman, I. (1985) 'Using health promotion to reduce alcohol problems' in Grant, M. (ed) (1985) *Alcohol Policies,* Geneva: WHO.

Simpson, R. and Isaac, S. (1982) *On Selecting a Definition for Health Promotion* Addiction Research Foundation.

Tones, K. (1981) 'Affective education and health', in David, K. and Williams, T. (eds) (1981) *Health Education in Schools,* London: Harper and Row.

Weir, K. (1992) 'Health promotion: the contribution of education' in MacDonald and Bunton (1992).

Governors and Parents

Ann Holt

'It takes a whole village to raise a child', says an old African proverb. In our own complex and differentiated communities the truth of the proverb is no less recognisable but will certainly take more effort to achieve. In recent years much of the government rhetoric surrounding education has emphasised the role of parents and the wider community in the upbringing and education of young people and the need for strategies that enable people to pull together. In the government white paper *Choice and Diversity* the government's own education priorities – quality, choice, diversity, autonomy and accountability – are to be achieved not by teachers alone, but also through 'action by governors, the initiative of parents, new legislation' (DfE, 1992, para.1.67).

We can assume then, that just as parents and the community are important for broad education policy, they are important for particular aspects such as the priority of developing a health promotion policy, so much favoured by the Department of Health (1992) in *The Health of the Nation*.

The Governing Body – a new focus

'The objective has been both to put governing bodies and headteachers under the greater pressure of public accountability for better standards and to increase their freedom to respond to that pressure ... It is that combination of unpaid but increasingly experienced governors and professional senior staff that is best placed to ... meet parents' wishes generally' (DfE, 1992, para.2.8).

There can be no doubt that the new style governing body in power since 1988, is a forum where the views and aspirations for a school of the community, and of parents in particular, can be shared and acted upon. If health education is to be a curriculum priority then a governing body must be convinced. Parental demand would certainly be one way of convincing it but there may be something of a chicken and egg situation here whereby the governing body may be an agent for convincing the parent body that health education is crucial.

The Governing Body – roles and responsibilities

In whatever way the notion of developing a health education curriculum reaches the governing body agenda, through parents, staff or interested governors, the governing body will have five basic roles to fulfil. It has to:

- bring together and discuss the range of views seen from the variety of perspectives on the governing body;

- decide priorities and make a policy;
- advise the head, staff and parents of that policy;
- support and promote the policy by adequately resourcing it with materials and staff;
- monitor the implementation of the policy and adapt it if necessary.

Within the statutory responsibilities of the governing body, there is ample scope for health education to be given time, space and consideration. The governing body has responsibility for the overall vision, mission and aims of the school and for its ethos and curriculum in particular. Specifically within that overall responsibility it has to:

- produce a statement of curriculum aims which includes the National Curriculum but is not exclusively the National Curriculum;
- engage with the process of creating a school development plan;
- control the budgeting and staffing of a school;
- make a policy for sex education.

Sex Education – a way in for governors

Since the Education (No 2) Act (1986) governing bodies have had the responsibility to consider and decide what a school will do about sex education and to keep the matter under review. Practice on this is not always good. Many schools still have no policy and others have paperwork which is out of date or bears no resemblance to what actually happens. The 1993 Education Act makes sex education in secondary schools compulsory from September 1994. Primary schools have the option to make their policy not to do it. Whatever the policy, parents will have the right to withdraw their children if they are not happy (see also Chapter 2).

Most parents will not want to exercise this option if governing bodies follow the advice of Circular 11/86 (DES, 1986) and which will remain in the new circular – namely to place their teaching:

'in a clear moral framework, important aspects being self-restraint, dignity, respect for themselves and others, the benefits of stable married and family life and the responsibilities of parenthood'.

Governors would be foolish to produce a sex education policy in a vacuum without consulting parents and teachers. To do so would mean that the policy would almost certainly remain in the drawer, unused. Effective policies need the consent and the compliance of all the partners.

Since good sex education is that which is provided in the context of good health education and, in turn, within the context of a health promoting school, it is clearly a most appropriate way in for looking at the place of a full-blown health education curriculum.

Some pointers for the policy-making process

- Take account of wider curricular considerations including:
  - (a) an overview of relevant legislation;
  - (b) religious and cultural factors present within the school and the wider community.
- Provide clear aims, objectives and guidelines for teachers and parents.
- Work at genuine acceptance and ownership by the key participants: governors, parents, pupils, teachers and other members of the community, eg school nurse, GP, religious leaders.
- Provide adequate resources and in-service training.
- Monitor the use and progress of the policy.

Possible headlines for a policy

- **WHAT?**   Content and resources
- **WHO?**   Teacher selection and modes of delivery
- **WHERE?**   Curriculum plan and health across the curriculum
- **WHEN?**   Content related to age groups
- **WHO?**   Teaching methodology

A process for policy development

Education session – awareness raising/motivating

Formation of working party

Draft policy

Consultation on draft policy

Final policy

Ratification

Education to support implementation of policy

Evaluation of effectiveness

A Hierarchy of the Needs and Strengths of Parents

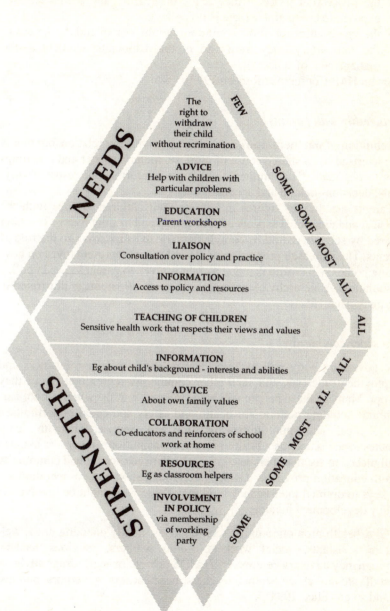

Figure 3 A hierarchy of the needs and strengths of parents (from Atkin and Bastiani, 1988)

Governing bodies, by producing a health education policy, are part of:

- the **consent** arrangements (they legitimise the actions of the head-teacher and staff);
- the **protection** process (they leave the teacher and pupils unfairly exposed to complaint if there is no policy);
- the **representation** of the community to the school and the school to the community (they form part of the democratic element in the management of schools);

(from an HMI Conference Report, 1992).

Partnership with parents

A definition of **partnership** (Pugh, 1989) is a working relationship that is characterised by: a shared sense of purpose, mutual respect and a willingness to negotiate. This implies a sharing of: information; responsibility; skills; decision-making and accountability.

Parents are the key figures in helping their children to cope with the physical and emotional aspects of growing up and healthy living. Teaching offered by schools should be complementary and supportive to the role of parents. The increased proportion of elected parent representatives on governing bodies will ensure that due weight is given to parent views in policy formulation. A hierarchy of strengths and needs of parents is illustrated in Figure 3, page 155.

The wider community

The governing body will include local political, religious, business and employment interests, and such other community representatives as they co-opt. Many of these people will have an interest in the wider school curriculum including policies for health and safety and equal opportunities, school meals and opportunities for sport and exercise. All of this contributes to the school as a health promoting institution. Governors are also well placed to see that there is consonance between school and community health education provision. Contact, communication and co-operation are all keys to optimal inter-agency working. Those who might be involved in policy development include:

GPs, health promotion units, school nurses, family planning units, welfare assistants, social workers, youth workers, religious leaders, pregnancy advisory centres, HIV/AIDS prevention staff, drugs advisory staff, alcohol abuse centres, teachers, headteachers, governors, parents, and so on (Flux, 1994).

Conclusion

Integral to sound health education is the skill to choose well – to choose to live healthily. Not only will the school want to make space for this to be addressed in the curriculum but the whole life of the school will present opportunities for the exercise of health-giving choices. In the Reith Lectures of 1990, Rabbi Jonathan Sachs said:

> 'Without the communities that sustain it, there is no such thing as private virtue. Instead, there is individualism: the self as consumer and chooser. And the free market can be a very harsh place for those who make the wrong choices ... In an individualistic culture, prizes are not evenly distributed. They go to those with supportive relationships: to those, in particular, with strong families and communities'.

In health terms, we could interpret it this way: with all the temptations, whether from drugs, alcohol, smoking, unsafe sex, over-eating, or little exercise – you name it – to make unhealthy choices, the individual pupil as consumer is up against it. It will take a concerted effort on the part of the school, the parents and the community, pulling in the same direction, to make health education in the curriculum a priority, and for our young people to become adult in their choices about health. 'It takes a whole village to raise a child.'

References

Atkin, J. and Bastiani, J. (1988) *Listening to Parents* London: Croom Helm.
Christians in Education (1992) *Guidelines for Developing a Sex Education Policy: a resource document for teachers and school governors* London: CARE.
Department for Education (DfE) (1992) *Choice and Diversity: a new framework for schools* London: HMSO.
Flux, A. and Flux, R. (1994) *Our Sexual Health Charter* London: State of Flux.
HMI (1992) *Drawing the Lines: Conference Report* London: DfE.
Pugh, G. in Wolfendale, S. (ed) (1989) *Parental Involvement: developing networks between home, school and communities*, London: Cassell.

Address

Christians in Education (CiE) and CARE: 53 Romney Street, London SW1 3RF.

The Influence of the Media

Roger Dickinson

Health and the issues surrounding it have pervaded the mass media for many years. The treatment of illness and disease, medical research, the costs of health care and the role of government, work and leisure and their links with personal health and well-being are not only frequent topics for news coverage, but are also the subject of regular feature articles in newspapers and magazines, and provide the subject matter for numerous radio and television programmes, ranging from soap operas and situation comedies to current affairs programmes and documentaries. At the same time the press and television abound with advertisements for foods, drinks and products associated with personal or household hygiene. The ubiquity of health in the mass media seems reason enough to assume that they play a significant role in shaping our health behaviour.

For those with responsibility for health education the media are clearly a force to be reckoned with. A look at what the media actually offer should alert those interested in developing and implementing health education initiatives to just how important an influence they are.

Health educators often see the media as allies because they can reach large numbers of people. Public communication campaigns on specific behaviours such as smoking, drug or alcohol use, use the media to reach the whole population or carefully target specific audiences: smokers, young people, or parents, for example. The underlying belief is that the media can be used to persuade people to alter their behaviour – to give up bad habits and adopt new, healthier life-styles.

Despite this optimism research has shown that the media are not especially effective by themselves in bringing about changes in people's health behaviour. The process of media influence is rather complex and the media's power to directly affect attitudes and behaviour is limited by a whole range of factors. Our family, neighbourhood, community, workplace or school relationships are at least as influential as the media. Because of this direct, persuasive media messages are unlikely to bring about measurable changes in public health (Rice and Atkin, 1989; Atkin and Wallack, 1990).

But this is not to say that the media have no influence. They have, but they exert it unevenly and indirectly. They probably have their greatest impact in raising public awareness about new issues and by conveying simple information. Communications researchers now believe that the media's power is exercised most through their capacity to 'set the agenda' for public debate about current issues and ideas, telling us not so much **what** to believe, but what issues are important and how we should think about them. The media seem to contribute to the general climate of opinion in which certain ideas, pieces of information, points of view, and models for behaviour are given prominence over others. How or indeed whether this results in action on our part depends on our particular circumstances, but our ideas and expectations about most social issues, including health, are probably very greatly affected by the media. The media and those other sources of influence act together to shape our behaviour.

There are four main ways in which the media portray health (Karpf, 1988). There is the **medical** approach which emphasises the role of the medical profession and the use of high-tech medical treatments. Then there is the **consumer** approach which takes the patients' view in the doctor–patient relationship. This contrasts with the **look-after-yourself** approach where attention is directed to individual behaviour and personal responsibility – the approach implicit in most school and public health education initiatives. A fourth approach explores the wider societal or **environmental** causes of ill-health and disease, such as poor housing and working conditions, industrial pollution, and the activities of big business.

This typology is useful when trying to assess the media's influence on health. Studies show that the medical approach dominates media coverage of health issues. This is especially the case in news coverage and in documentaries where doctors (who are usually men) are traditionally depicted as powerful, dominant, successful, and sociable individuals battling against disease and using the good of medicine to triumph, often via some spectacular intervention or other (the life-saving operation, for example), over the recalcitrant evils of nature. This tradition began with television programmes like *Your Life in Their Hands* in the 1950s, and continues today in programmes like *Horizon* and *Tomorrow's World* which regularly feature path-breaking medical scientists. This image of health also appears frequently in the popular press. Medical authority – the power to define a health problem and its solution – is rarely questioned in this type of health coverage.

The medical approach also tends to prevail in television fiction. When doctors appear they are there to dispense wisdom and reason, and frequently step in to provide the salve of rationality to the chaotic human condition. This is the role of the local GP in *Emmerdale* or *EastEnders*, for instance.

So despite programmes like *That's Life* or *Watchdog* which are sometimes critical of the medical profession, or programmes like *Where There's Life* or the BBC special all-evening *Health Show* which invite us to take charge of ourselves and our bodies, television encourages us to think of health mainly in terms of curative medicine.

Programmes addressing broader concerns are unusual, and tend to be documentaries rather than popular series. The recent Channel 4 series *The Food File*, for example, dealt critically with the food industry. *Equinox* on the same channel takes a sceptical view of science in general, and occasionally of medicine in particular. The BBC series *Casualty*, with its continuing theme of hard pressed staff struggling against the tide of NHS spending cuts is a very rare example of popular drama as social commentary.

But this environmental approach to health so rarely gets an airing in the media that the public seldom have the opportunity to understand the underlying social, economic and political causes of ill-health. The media merely help to perpetuate the medical model of health care, sometimes showing how marginal improvements can be made to standards of care, and occasionally offering pointers to self-improvement. The reasons why the medical model dominates are complex, but an important factor is the powerful position of medical science in contemporary society, and in particular the power enjoyed by the medical profession itself to shape the coverage it receives (Turow, 1989; Nelkin, 1987).

Whatever the dominant model of health on offer, however, it is clear that the media present a number of confusing and contradictory images of health. We see doctors in television drama offering miracle cures alongside news images of overworked hospital medics whose fallibility is revealed in stories of the latest medical blunder or case of malpractice; we see characters casually consuming unhealthy foods, spending a large proportion of their leisure time in pubs or cafés, and taking little exercise (with no apparent ill-effects) alongside documentaries exploring the latest techniques in heart by-pass surgery; we can learn new ways to cook the Sunday roast on daytime television and later in the evening watch an exposé of the grim realities of factory farming; and we see non-nutritious foods – mostly snacks and sweets – being eaten by slim, fit and energetic-looking characters, as if food intake were unrelated to body weight (Kaufman, 1980).

Many of these images compromise and compete with health education's look-after-yourself health messages. Some health educators have reacted to this by lobbying the government and the media industry for tighter controls over media output, and calling for more 'responsible' portrayal of health issues (Montgomery, 1987). For example, broadcasters were asked recently to limit the amount of food advertising on children's television (Dibb, 1993). For several years the anti-smoking movement has been active in trying to persuade the television industry to boycott tobacco-sponsored sport and thereby stop providing free television advertising for the major tobacco brands.

Most western governments already restrict paid tobacco and alcohol advertising, and the producers of popular television drama programmes now make sure that all their characters are non-smokers, and restrict alcohol consumption on screen. But programmes like *EastEnders, Coronation Street,* and *Emmerdale* are difficult to imagine without the comings and goings at the local pub. It is equally difficult to think of television schedules without at least one medical drama featuring a benign, authoritative doctor dispensing wisdom, compassion, and **medical** expertise. Medical documentaries, though occasionally critical and questioning, seem likely to continue to engender a belief that one day, given sufficient research funding, all forms of ill-health and disease will be curable. Other, less frequent programmes will meanwhile urge us to control our diet and take more exercise while we wait for cures to be discovered. Media coverage of the environmental causes of ill-health is likely to be the exception rather than the rule.

So, while lobbyists press broadcasters to remove negative role models from soap operas, regulate food advertising and help keep sport free from 'unhealthy' sponsorship, the general pattern of the media's coverage of health will probably continue. Confused and confusing but overwhelmingly **medical** in their message – a message which those responsible for the delivery of health education, whatever the context, would do well to recognise.

References

Atkin, C. and Wallack, L. (eds) (1990) *Mass Communication and Public Health: Complexities and Conflicts* London: Sage Publications.

Dibb, S. (1993) *Children: Advertiser's Dream, Nutrition Nightmare* London: National Food Alliance.

Karpf, A. (1988) *Doctoring the Media: The Reporting of Health and Medicine* London: Routledge.

Kaufman, L. (1980) 'Prime-time nutrition', *Journal of Communication,* **30** (3), 37–46.

Montgomery, K. (1987) *Target: Prime Time. Advocacy Groups and the Struggle Over Entertainment Television* New York: Oxford University Press.

Nelkin, D. (1987) *Selling Science: How the Press Covers Science and Technology* New York: WH Freeman.

Rice, R. and Atkin, C. (eds) (1989) *Public Communication Campaigns* London: Sage Publications.

Turow, J. (1989) *Playing Doctor: Television, Storytelling and Medical Power* New York: Oxford University Press.

Index

Abortion 14-15, 81
AIDS (Acquired Immune Deficiency Syndrome) 9, 12-14, 16, 35, 47, 81, 88, 103, 130, 149, 156
Alcohol 13, 15, 31, 36, 39, 41, 43, 66, 79, 97, 130, 156
Assessment 3, 52-54
Bullying 54, 143
Cancer 9, 25, 27, 30, 32-34
Choice 4-5, 10, 15, 18-19, 47, 50, 63, 65, 71, 80, 89, 91, 97, 115, 125-127, 129-130, 138, 143-145, 157
Communication skill 12, 40, 43, 135
Community 2-5, 10-11, 13, 16-17, 19-21, 26, 54, 59, 61, 66, 71, 89, 96, 105, 112-113, 126, 142-145, 148, 152, 154, 156-157
Contraception 15, 35, 81, 98
Decision-making 105, 108, 125, 129, 131, 133-135, 138, 145, 156
Drugs 10, 14-15, 36, 44, 79, 96, 98, 102, 130, 139-140, 156
Environmental 13, 19, 25, 36, 57, 62, 70-72, 80, 92-93, 108, 118, 139, 144, 159-161
Ethos 1, 4-5, 54, 67, 122, 131, 153
European Network 20-21
Family 4, 14, 26, 37, 66, 75, 84-85, 90-91, 97-98, 111, 116, 126-127, 131, 134, 153
Food 4, 18, 31, 65, 71, 78, 84-85, 96-97, 101-102, 116, 133, 138-139, 144-145, 158-161
Governor 14, 53-54, 123, 144, 150, 152-154, 156-157
Health authority 148-149, 151
Health career 11, 15
Health education co-ordinator 11, 80, 82
Health professional 6, 12, 17, 27, 82, 135, 142-145
Health promoting school 5, 17-21, 67, 112, 142-143, 153
Health Trust 77, 145
Health promotion 5-6, 8, 10, 13, 16, 18, 21, 24-27, 36-37, 102-103, 110, 143, 147-150, 152, 156
Health-related behaviour 9, 41, 126
Health-related exercise 4, 102, 110, 116
Heart disease 9, 13, 16, 26, 29-30, 111
Hidden curriculum 5, 15, 18, 122
HIV (Human Immunodeficiency Virus) 35, 47-50, 81, 102, 130, 149, 156
Hygiene 4, 8, 47, 79, 101-103, 116, 118, 138, 142, 150, 158
Life skills 8, 12, 15, 59
Life-style 8-9, 14-16, 18, 20, 24-25, 27, 32, 50, 53, 65-66, 70-72, 79, 96, 101, 110-112, 126, 129-130, 137, 148
Mental 1, 5, 10, 34, 52, 111
Moral 11, 15, 39, 43, 47, 66-67, 81, 120, 122-123, 125, 153
National Health Service (NHS) 26, 29, 34, 57-58, 65, 80, 105, 127, 148, 160
Nutrition 4, 17, 57, 84-86, 93, 101-102, 116, 134, 139, 142, 144
Parent 2, 6, 9, 11-12, 14, 17, 19, 37, 43, 50, 53, 58, 77-78, 82, 123, 129-130, 135, 144-145, 150, 152-157, 158
Peer 10-11, 19, 29, 31, 36, 41-44, 54, 70, 87, 104, 111, 126, 130-131, 135, 150
Personal and social education (PSE) 11, 56, 63, 79, 111
Problem-solving 1, 12, 42, 44, 61, 74, 102
Psychological 4, 18-19, 37, 66, 70, 115-116, 125, 127, 140
Racism 54, 138
Risk factor 9-10, 16, 26
Safety 4, 36, 49-50, 57-58, 62-63, 66, 77, 79-80, 84-85, 97, 101-103, 107, 116, 127, 143, 156
Self-esteem 16, 20, 39, 42-43, 67, 103, 107, 110-111, 113, 115-117, 129-131, 133-135
Sensitive issues 41-42, 54, 130
Sex education 4, 12, 14-15, 18-19, 41, 53, 80-81, 102-103, 117, 120, 123, 129-131, 150, 153
Sexual health 4, 14, 35, 143, 149, 151
Smoking 16, 18-19, 24-25, 27, 29-30, 32, 40-41, 44, 57-59, 62, 66, 70, 102, 105, 127, 130-131, 137, 157, 158
Stereotyping 17, 54, 127
Television 43, 105, 158-161
Values 4-5, 10, 13, 15, 19, 40, 45, 50, 58, 64, 66-67, 71, 81, 84, 89, 103, 105, 107, 110, 120, 122-123, 129, 135, 138
World Health Organisation (WHO) 13, 17-19, 21, 23, 65, 147-148